# THE CHRONICLES OF NARNIA

*The Patterning of a Fantastic World*

TWAYNE'S MASTERWORK STUDIES:
CHILDREN'S AND YOUNG ADULT
LITERATURE

*Robert Lecker, General Editor*

# THE CHRONICLES OF NARNIA

## The Patterning of a Fantastic World

Colin Manlove

TWAYNE PUBLISHERS • NEW YORK
Maxwell Macmillan Canada • Toronto
Maxwell Macmillan International • New York Oxford Singapore Sydney

*Twayne's Masterwork Studies No. 127*

*The Chronicles of Narnia: The Patterning of a Fantastic World*
Colin Manlove

Twayne Publishers                       Maxwell Macmillan Canada, Inc.
Macmillan Publishing Company            1200 Eglinton Avenue East
866 Third Avenue                        Suite 200
New York, New York 10022                Don Mills, Ontario M3C 3N1

**Library of Congress Cataloging-in-Publication Data**

Manlove, C. N. (Colin Nicholas), 1942–
    The chronicles of Narnia : the patterning of a fantastic world /
Colin Manlove.
        p.   cm.—(Twayne's masterwork studies. Children's and young
adult literature ; no. 1)
    Includes bibliographical references and index.
    ISBN 0-8057-8800-X (alk. paper).—ISBN 0-8057-8801-8 (pbk. :
alk. paper)
    1. Lewis, C. S. (Clive Staples), 1898–1963. Chronicles of Narnia.
    2. Children's stories, English—History and criticism.   3. Fantastic
fiction, English—History and criticism.   I. Title.   II. Series.
PR6023.E926C536   1993
823'.912—dc20                                                    92-46286
                                                                      CIP

The paper used in this publication meets the minimum requirements of American
National Standard for Information Sciences—Permanence of Paper for Printed
Library Materials. ANSI Z3948-1984.⊚™

10  9  8  7  6  5  4  3  2  1 (hc)
10  9  8  7  6  5  4  3  2  1 (pb)

Printed in the United States of America

For Hilary and Edward

# CONTENTS

# ILLUSTRATIONS

C. S. Lewis in 1947. Copyright Arthur Strong. Reprinted by permission.

# NOTE ON THE REFERENCES AND ACKNOWLEDGMENTS

Throughout, references are to the Puffin editions of the novels (Harmondsworth, Middlesex: Penguin): *The Lion, the Witch and the Wardrobe* (1959), *Prince Caspian* (1962), *The Voyage of the "Dawn Treader"* (1965), *The Silver Chair* (1965), *The Horse and His Boy* (1965), *The Magician's Nephew* (1963), and *The Last Battle* (1964).

I am grateful to Arthur Strong for permission to reproduce the photograph of C. S. Lewis, and to Penguin Books for permission to reproduce Pauline Baynes' map of Narnia.

I would like to thank two people from Twayne Publishers who had a particular part in making this book: editor Sylvia K. Miller to whom I am indebted for numerous creative suggestions and copyeditor Melissa Dobson for a most searching overhaul of the typescript.

# CHRONOLOGY:
## C. S. LEWIS'S LIFE AND WORKS

| | |
|---|---|
| 1898 | Clive Staples Lewis is born on 29 November in Belfast to Albert James Lewis, a police-court solicitor, and Flora Augusta Hamilton Lewis, a university-educated woman with an honors degree in mathematics, exceptional for a woman at that time. |
| 1898–1908 | Lewis enjoys a happy and increasingly well-to-do childhood in Belfast. In 1905 begins with his brother, W. H. "Warnie" Lewis, the tales of "Animal-land," which will later develop into the chronicles of "Boxen." |
| 1908 | Flora Lewis dies of cancer. Albert's grief and violent behavior subsequent to her death have lasting impact on Lewis, who is sent to Wynard House, a boarding school near London run by a sadistic headmaster, the Reverend Robert Capron, nicknamed "Oldie." |
| 1911–1913 | Attends Cherbourg preparatory school, where he loses his family-instilled Ulster Protestant faith. |
| 1913–1914 | Attends Malvern College and is unhappy, largely due to importance placed there on success in sports. |
| 1914–1917 | Educated privately by his father's former teacher, William T. Kirkpatrick, "the Great Knock." This is a highly demanding education in languages, particularly the classics, and literature, and Lewis is an exemplary student. |
| 1916 | Happens upon George MacDonald's *Phantastes*. Later he will declare that this book "baptized" his imagination. Takes scholarship examination for Oxford in December and is accepted by University College. |
| 1917 | Volunteers for service in World War I. Begins military training in the summer, after one term at Oxford. Befriends fellow cadet Paddy Moore, and through him Moore's 45-year-old mother. |
| 1917–1918 | Stationed in Flanders from November to April, when he is hospitalized with shrapnel wound and returns to England. |

|           | Paddy Moore killed in action. Lewis fulfills pledge to look after his mother; the relationship between them probably becomes sexual. |
|-----------|---|
| 1919 | *Spirits in Bondage*, Lewis's first book (poetry) is published by Heinemann under the name Clive Hamilton. |
| 1919–1922 | Returns to Oxford and reads Classics at University College, earning First Class Honors degree. Lives with Mrs. Moore, but is financially supported by his father throughout, despite strained relations. |
| 1922–1923 | Reads English at Oxford and earns second First Class degree. |
| 1923–1924 | Attempts to secure a university teaching post are unsuccessful. |
| 1924–1925 | Holds temporary lectureship in philosophy at University College, Oxford. |
| 1925 | Accepts fellowship in English Language and Literature at Magdalen College, Oxford. (Retains position to 1954.) |
| 1926 | Has first meeting with J. R. R. Tolkien in May. Lewis's long poem *Dymer* is published in July, but disappointing critical reception thwarts his central ambition as a poet. |
| 1929 | Lewis converts to theism in the summer. Albert Lewis dies in September. |
| 1930 | Lewis and Mrs. Moore buy a house, the Kilns, in North Oxford, with the help of his brother, Warnie, who moves in with them in 1932. |
| 1931 | Lewis returns to Christianity. |
| 1933 | *The Pilgrim's Regress* is published. |
| 1936 | *The Allegory of Love* is published by Oxford University Press under the editorship of Charles Williams, whose *The Place of the Lion* (1931) Lewis is then enthusiastically reading. The two meet and become friends. The "Inklings" group—its central figures Lewis, Williams, and Tolkien, with Owen Barfield and Hugo Dyson—begins meeting about this time (to 1949), to sustain and encourage its members' mythopoeic writings. |
| 1938 | *Out of the Silent Planet* (the first book of Lewis's space trilogy) is published. This, and to a greater extent Lewis's and Tolkien's backing of an unsuitable candidate for the Oxford Chair of Poetry, begin to harm Lewis's reputation at Oxford. |
| 1939 | Charles Williams is evacuated to Oxford with the London Branch of Oxford University Press as a consequence of World War II; a close friendship develops between Williams and Lewis. |
| 1940 | *The Problem of Pain* (apologetics) is published. |

# Chronology

1941    Lewis begins Christian radio talks and tours England speaking to servicemen.

1942    *The Screwtape Letters: Letters from a Senior to a Junior Devil,* Lewis's most popular book (apologetics), and *A Preface to "Paradise Lost"* are published.

1943    *Perelandra* (the second book of the space trilogy) is published. Lewis's colleagues become inreasingly hostile to his popular success.

1945    Charles Williams dies in May. *That Hideous Strength* (final book of the space trilogy) is published in July, followed by *The Great Divorce* in November.

1947    *Miracles* (apologetics) is published in May. Lewis is rejected for the Merton Chair of English Literature at Oxford.

1948    Defeated by the philosopher Elizabeth Anscombe in a celebrated debate over Lewis's *Miracles* at the Oxford Socratic Club. Gradual cooling of friendship with Tolkien.

1950–1956    The *Chronicles of Narnia* are published.

1951    Mrs. Moore dies in January after long period of invalidity, ending Lewis's responsibility for her care; but Warnie, now an alcoholic, remains a demand on Lewis's care. In February Lewis is nominated for the Oxford Chair of Poetry and is narrowly defeated by Cecil Day-Lewis.

1952    Meets Joy Gresham (née Davidman), an American writer who had been corresponding with him since 1950. (Joy moves to England with her two sons in 1953.) *Mere Christianity* is published.

1954    Lewis's classic *Oxford History of English Literature in the Sixteenth Century, Excluding Drama* is published. Lewis is appointed Professor of Medieval and Renaissance English Literature at the University of Cambridge.

1956    Marries Joy Gresham on 23 April. *Till We Have Faces: A Myth Retold* is published. In October, Joy diagnosed as having breast cancer.

1957    Joy makes apparently miraculous recovery. Lewis is increasingly estranged from his male friends.

1959    Joy again diagnosed with cancer in October. She and Lewis vacation in Greece, Lewis's first trip abroad since his wartime service in 1917–1918.

1960    Joy dies on 14 July. Lewis writes *A Grief Observed,* a moving treatment of loss that is a contrast to the more facile *The Problem of Pain.* (This is published in 1961 under the auspices of T. S. Eliot, then managing director of Faber and Faber, with whom Lewis had never "got on.")

1961–1962     Enjoys happy years at Cambridge. Writes *An Experiment in Criticism*, attacking F. R. Leavis's "evaluative" approach to, and "over-serious" criticism of, literature. Suffers from an enlarged prostate and, under dubious medical care, wears a crude catheter from 1962 which finally ruins his health.

1962–1963     Last meeting, one winter day, with Tolkien. The relationship is by this time impoverished.

1963     Retires from Cambridge post in August. Requires nursing care. Walter Hooper, a university student visiting from the United States, becomes his secretary. Lewis dies on 22 November. Warnie is with him in his last minutes.

*Literary and Historical Context*

# 1

## Historical Context

C. S. Lewis in his life and work stood apart from, at times opposed to, the culture and milieu of his day. In the august setting of his inaugural lecture as Professor of Medieval and Renaissance Literature at the University of Cambridge in 1955, Lewis proclaimed himself an "Old Western Man," a cultural "dinosaur," the exponent of values, both literary and moral, which he believed had died out about 1830.[1] He knew little of modern literature apart from works that were akin to his own, particularly those of J. R. R. Tolkien and Charles Williams; he was put off by the poetry of T. S. Eliot, whose Christian work might be described as near to his in spirit. His kinship was with writers who look to the past, such as William Morris and even Sir Walter Scott, and with the genres of romance, saga, epic, and allegory, as seen in his fondness for Homer, Virgil, *Beowulf*, the Old Norse *Eddas*, Ludovico Ariosto, Edmund Spenser, and John Milton. He retained in his adult life a love for the children's literature that had inspired him as a boy—books by Robert Louis Stevenson, Edith Nesbit, Beatrix Potter, and Kenneth Grahame. Practically all his fiction expresses the desire to escape from the world; this is especially true of the Narnia books, which combine a wish to reenter childhood and a yearning for a simpler, more pastoral realm.

In Oxford, for all his gregariousness and his popularity as a lecturer, Lewis expressed the feeling of belonging "elsewhere." This feeling may have had its source in the lost idyll of his childhood, the time up to his mother's death in 1908 when Lewis was ten; it can also be traced to his lifelong fascination with "otherness," and even to his spiritual claustrophobia.[2] When Lewis returned to Christianity in 1931 he set out to suppress or sublimate whole areas of his emotional and physical nature as unpresentable to God.[3] After his conversion he grew increasingly alienated from his academic peers: they, while perhaps envious of his literary success, saw him as compromising his scholarly position through his popular Christian apologetics and the writing of fantasy.[4] He retained few academic friends at the Oxford college where he taught, Magdalen, or in the Oxford English faculty, and he increasingly looked to friendships elsewhere in Oxford with like-minded individuals such as Tolkien, Owen Barfield, and later, Charles Williams. This group, headed by Lewis, became the Inklings; its members pooled their varied interests in weekly meetings. Together with the Socratic Club, over which Lewis also presided, the Inklings represented Oxford's Christian voice, particularly during the Second World War years, when the issue of faith was quickened everywhere by danger. Certainly to Lewis such a group seemed an island of old values in an encroaching sea of liberal theology and humanism.[5]

As to the wider world (apart from its Christian condition), Lewis was largely indifferent to history and politics. There is little in his letters to indicate a preoccupation with any historical event, and the Second World War seems to have served only the function of enabling him through radio talks to instruct people on how to get their minds above the war. He was politically and socially ill-informed, and this contributed to a number of his prejudices. He rarely read the newspapers. He believed Tito to be king of Greece.[6] His psyche seemed to have been largely unaltered by the experience of having served in the trenches in the First World War (something that could not so readily be said of Tolkien). What impressed Lewis was his reading of the French philosopher Henri Bergson while he was in a convalescent camp on Salisbury Plain, or that through his experience of the war he was able to understand the philosopher Immanuel Kant's distinction between the "noumenal" and the "phenomenal."[7] It is thus faintly ironic that the day of Lewis's death coincided with a major historical event, the assassination of President John F. Kennedy.

But if Lewis was in this sense impervious to "life"—at least until Joy Gresham arrived on the scene—he was extremely permeable to books. Indeed, books and the mental life they stimulated became a substitute for experience. One of the most momentous events of his life, he tells us in the autobiographical *Surprised by Joy* 1955, was picking up a copy of George MacDonald's *Phantastes* in 1916 and reading it on a train: it "baptised" his imagination.[8] Remarkable in that autobiography is the perfunctory use of dates: like John Bunyan's *Grace Abounding*, Lewis's account is the history of a human spirit assailed by words and thoughts. MacDonald, Milton, Spenser, Homer, Virgil—these were influences on Lewis akin to marriage, divorce, war, and bereavement: they were events to him. (Curiously, the work of Tolkien is not an evident influence: it is as though with the Narnia books Lewis set out to write something entirely different from *The Lord of the Rings*, which he was even then reading and vastly enjoying.[9])

While Lewis paid little attention to current affairs, he was very much aware of what he saw as the dissolution of Christian belief in modern society. His fantasy can be seen as a response to what he perceived was an anti-theistic tendency in modern life (which may be why the Narnia stories begin in a contemporary setting). Because he sensed that Christianity's influence was ebbing, he was the more ardent in its defense, the more ready to expand its presence to planets and possible worlds. Because he himself had been an atheist, he believed he understood the forces arrayed against his late-won faith, and felt particularly equipped to take them on. Certainly as a writer of fantasy he is peculiarly an apologist.[10] His desire to convert, or at any rate to show the wonder of a divinely based universe, informs, directly or indirectly, nearly all his work. Anyone who has read *The Problem of Pain*, *Miracles*, or *Mere Christianity*, written not long before the Narnia volumes, knows the appeal of a mind seeming to work things out from first principles, giving full rein to skepticism before dispensing with it through an impressive display of reason and logic. Lewis was adept at constructing clinching analogies. Above all he had the capacity to be simple without being facile. Modified forms of many of these qualities, particularly his lack of condescension, served him well as a writer for children. We are, as it were, surprised into awareness of the divine resonances of *The Lion, the Witch and the Wardrobe*, and our experience of wonder is gradually tapered toward the mystical in *The Voyage of the "Dawn Treader."* Surprise, indeed, is almost the leitmotiv of Lewis's Christian and literary life: it lends a particular vividness to his writing.

Lewis does not, of course, argue any case in the *Chronicles of Narnia*: rather, he writes mythopoeia within a resonant literary and biblical tradition. The Christ story underlies the death and resurrection of Aslan in *The Lion;* the creation and the fall in Genesis inform *The Magician's Nephew*, and the apocalypse in Revelation is an analogue to the end of Narnia in *The Last Battle*. Lewis expected through myth—of which he found George MacDonald's work the finest example—not only to see the pattern of holiness, but to *feel* it.[11] One of the central threads of his "Romantic theology" is a belief that certain images may act as temporary vessels of God, filling human beings with a longing, or *Sehnsucht*, for heaven; this has its roots in such Romantic images of spiritual desire as Novalis's blue flower, Wordsworth's nature, and Shelley's fading coal. All his life he moved from image to image, experiencing the intermittent and random gleams of everlastingness.[12] And throughout his fiction he moved from imagined world to imagined world—Puritania, Malacandra, Perelandra, the purlieus of heaven, Narnia, Glome. All his fantasies are in some sense passing pictures of desire.

The Narnia books are a remarkable mixture of literary influences: in *The Lion, the Witch and the Wardrobe* alone, the Bible, Milton, and Spenser rub shoulders with Edith Nesbit, Hans Christian Andersen, and Beatrix Potter. We can readily list what Lewis got from each: the dynamics of children's interaction and the rules of magic from Nesbit, the vitality of animal characterization (especially of the Beavers) from Potter, the beauty and terror of the White Witch and the frozen nature of Narnia from Andersen's "The Snow Queen," and so on. But our main interest must be with the more general influence of such sources, in which the great and the small, the important and the apparently trivial, seem to coexist, even to be fused. Such a fusion of least and greatest, such disproportion, is of the idiom of Christianity itself. But here it helps to sustain belief in the childlike even while that is turning to matters more strange and sometimes more terrible than any child could face alone. And that is the crucial strength of Lewis's Narnia books: that they utilize child and animal characters and the creatures of folk and fairy tale, to re-create literary traditions whose deeper meanings might otherwise be inaccessible.

Lewis may be the last significant writer of Christian fantasy, in a tradition extending back to the French *Queste del Saint Graal* (1215–30) and Dante's *Commedia* (1307–21). The object of such fantasy is to recreate Christian supernatural truth within an invented world.[13] That Lewis was able to do this so successfully at a time when the fantasy genre had become largely devoid of Christian sentiment, and the historical context in which he wrote was becoming ever more secularized, is a measure not only of his skill but of the conviction of his vision.

# 2

# *The Importance of the* Chronicles

Appearing in the early 1950s, the Narnia books represented a quite startling transformation of children's literature after the relative doldrums of the 1940s. They helped begin a renaissance in children's literature, and to some extent reassured librarians and schoolteachers, who had for too long to contend with the popularity of such authors as W. E. Johns (of the "Biggles" books), or the multitudinous and too-readily digested works of Enid Blyton, of the potency of the genre. More specifically, together with the work of Tolkien, Lewis's books ushered in the present popularity of the genre of fantasy.

The *Chronicles of Narnia* represented a return to the scope of children's fantasy seen in the work of Charles Kingsley, George Mac-Donald, Rudyard Kipling, and John Masefield. With their use of covert Christian themes and their admission of profound topics of sacrifice, death and resurrection, the nature of evil, the measure of faith, the divine creation and ending of a world, and the quest for the divine, they bring into children's literature an "adult" profundity of which it had long been felt incapable. Nor is this done awkwardly. The living strength of the *Chronicles* is in the way that such profundity is integrated with vivid child characters and adventures, so that it is possible

to read the narrative without becoming aware of any further significance, and likewise, when made aware of that significance, to be the
more deeply affected by it through the very surprise of its presence.
Beyond this, the *Chronicles* are profoundly *literary*, both in the way
that (unlike most other children's books) they draw naturally on the
great cultural tradition of Homer, Virgil, Dante, Spenser, Shakespeare,
Milton, and Bunyan, and in the clarity and complexity of their style
and form. Lewis maintained that he did not did not write specifically
for children at all, but wrote in the fairy-tale mode because, as the title
of one of his essays has it, "Sometimes Fairy Stories May Say Best
What's to Be Said." Before Lewis, whether in William Thackeray's
*The Rose and the Ring*, Lewis Carroll's "Alice" books, Mary Moles-
worth's *The Cuckoo Clock*, Kenneth Grahame's *The Golden Age* and
*The Wind in the Willows*, Edith Nesbit's magic books, Sir James
Barrie's *Peter Pan*, A. A. Milne's "Pooh" books, or Arthur Ransome's
stories, the reader had been asked to enter a child's world; now the
child's world was entering that of the adult reader. If there is any final
ethic that is taught by Lewis's books out of this, it is that nothing is
"mere." The apparently small—a fairy tale, a little world called Narnia, a group of contemporary children—can contain the very large
(just as, in *The Last Battle*, a stable is seen as once having contained
the entire world).[1] Lewis deliberately startles us into awareness by the
very abruptness with which his child characters become great heroic
figures in Narnia. In essay after essay after essay he makes war against
dismissive attitudes toward children's literature: " 'Juveniles,' indeed!
Am I to patronize sleep because children sleep sound? Or honey because children like it?"[2] After Lewis children's literature was not, and
was not seen to be, quite so provincial again.

Lewis, anticipated somewhat by Tolkien in *The Hobbit*, began a
tradition of "alternative world" fiction, the creation of an "other"
universe or land with its own history and geography. Of course there
are precedents in earlier literature, in Jonathan Swift, Bulwer Lytton,
David Lindsay, and E. R. Eddison: but there one finds less direct
concern with the making of a world for its own sake. Lewis exploits
the idea that God may have created many alternative natures, to which
our world would be as fantastic as theirs is to us. Within those "hetero-

# 3

## Critical Reception

For all their wide and continuing popularity, the *Chronicles of Narnia* have not received much more than coterie critical and scholarly attention so far. This may be attributable to the enduring academic prejudice against "popular" genres such as fantasy, science fiction, and children's literature; it may equally be assigned to the prevalent assumption that children's literature is by definition obvious, simplistic, and shallow. It is possible that recent critical theories favoring the widening of the canon will alter this, but to date it has been women's, rather than children's fiction that has benefited from the new zeal, which is in any case as much ideological as it is literary.

The critical response to the *Chronicles* since their publication has not always been evolutionary. Lewis studies generally have been bedeviled by "thematic" criticism; that is, the extraction of an author's ideas from his or her work. Lewis's ideas, thus extracted, often seem flat and clinical, lacking the impact they carry within the work. This approach has been taken by American Christian critics, who tend sometimes to treat the texts as near-religious experiences. Only since the 1980s, possibly since the publication of Peter Schakel's *Reading with the Heart: The Way into Narnia* (1979), has attention to the

*Chronicles* as literature really been paid. There is now an emerging sense that only by treating the books as imbued with complex and subtle artistic patterns, and not as mere components of a weltanschauung, will the true range of Lewis's ideas come forward. The act of literary criticism then becomes in tune with the idiom of reality as Lewis saw it, whereby what seems random is actually part of a far deeper pattern.

The vast bulk of criticism of Lewis (as of Tolkien and indeed almost any writer of fantasy or science fiction) has come from the United States. This perhaps reflects a more unabashedly Christian spirit in that land; but it also emerges from a far more democratic approach to literature in our transatlantic cousins. There are hundreds of courses in fantasy and science fiction in American colleges and universities, compared with the handful in the rainy little nook from which much of the material for these courses has emerged. Still, we begin here with the British response, which is at least able to be critical of Lewis. Lewis's close friend Tolkien found it almost unendurable to have a dose of Narnia administered to him every Thursday night at the meetings of the Inklings: he regarded *The Lion, the Witch and the Wardrobe* as put together out of too many ill-assorted pieces to make up a viable "sub-creation" (a self-consistent invented world), and also disliked its allegory; nor did he change his views with the rest of the series.[1] Nevertheless, encouraged by his friend Roger Lancelyn Green, who even allowed Lewis to recycle in his work his own unpublished *The Wood That Time Forgot*, Lewis pressed ahead to publication.[2]

Lewis saw the initial reaction to *The Lion* as hostile: "A number of mothers, and still more, schoolmistresses, have decided it is likely to frighten children, so it is not selling very well. But the real children like it, and I am astonished how some *very* young ones seem to understand it."[3] Lewis felt children were his best critics: his *Letters to Children* are full of his delight at their enthusiasm and interest. He replied to adult criticism of the works in a 1952 lecture at the Bournemouth Conference of the Library Association, "On Three Ways of Writing for Children," in which he defended fairy tales and the use, where necessary, of potentially frightening elements in them. According to R. L. Green, who was well acquainted with Lewis throughout this period, the Narnia books were attacked, variously, for not being "real-life" enough, for their Christianity, their violence, and their use of some unpleasant child characters.[4] The evidence compiled from the national reviews in the invaluable *Annotated Checklist* for C. S. Lewis by Joe R. Christopher and Joan K. Ostling (and further investigation by myself) is rather of general, if mild, enthusiasm from the outset, with intermittent attention from several leading British weekly journals such as the *Spectator, Times Literary Supplement,* and *New Statesman and Nation;* in the United States, Chad Walsh reviewed all seven books in the *New York Times Book Review.* Nevertheless the Narnia books received far fewer reviews than Lewis's earlier fiction. Several of the reviews are concerned with the vitality of the stories and characters in the books, and how effectively these go together with the deeper meanings. In 1956 the reviewer of *The Last Battle* in the Children's Books Section of the *Times Literary Supplement* for 11 May included the entire Narnian "saga" among the "greatest children's books."

Lewis had intended his books for a wide audience, though he would have been surprised by the scale of their eventual popularity. He might have been less ready for the explicators, source-hunters, and thesis writers who later began to move in; he always, out of modesty, tried to discourage scholarship about himself.[5] Nevertheless he praised the 1957 Long Beach Teachers College M. A. thesis of Kathryn A. Stillwell (later Lindskoog), "The Lion of Judah in Never-Never Land: The Theology and Philosophy of C. S. Lewis Expressed in His Fantasies for Children," for its sense of the relation of the books to the entire body of his work and to their sources in the Bible.[6] Most early treatments are in brief articles. Sources are suggested by Charles A. Brady (1956), Marcus Crouch (1962), and J. R. Christopher (1972); the geography of Narnia is explored by Crouch (1956), Glen Goodknight (1969), and J. R. Christopher (1971), who also investigates its cosmology and even its prehistory. There are American theses by Mary Burrows Thomas (1964; on the sources and meaning of the *Chronicles*), and by Jacqueline Foulon (1962) and Gloria Alfoja Cenit (1968), both attempting to show how the Narnia books may be used to teach Christian doctrine.[7] Walter Hooper's " 'Past Watchful Dragons': The Fairy Tales of C. S. Lewis" (1971; published separately under the same title by Collier of New York in 1979) provides a fine introduction, particularly useful in setting the *Chronicles* in the context of Lewis's ideas on fairy tales and myths, and in giving insights into their composition and chronology. The *Chronicles* are quickly subsumed into honored places in accounts of modern children's literature, as in Marcus Crouch's *Chosen for Children* (1957), Marjorie Fisher's *Intent upon Reading* (1961) and J. R. Townsend's *Written for Children* (1965). In 1969 a "Narnia Conference" was held in California, the proceedings of which were published in 1970. By this time the Lewis industry was in full gear, and the 1970s saw the establishment of several U.S. journals devoted wholly, or in part, to his work—*CSL: The Bulletin of the New York C. S. Lewis Society* (1969–), *The Chronicle of the Portland C. S. Lewis Society* (1972–), *Mythlore* (1973–), *The Lamp-post of the Southern California C. S. Lewis Society* (1974–), *The Canadian C. S. Lewis Journal* (1979–), and *Seven: An Anglo-American Literary Review* (1980–). All this in a context in which, as Walter Hooper pointed out in 1973, the *Chronicles of Narnia* were selling more than one million copies per year.[8]

For the main books on the *Chronicles of Narnia* we can start with Kathryn Lindskoog, *The Lion of Judah in Never-Never Land: The Theology of C. S. Lewis Expressed in His Fantasies for Children* (1973), the reworking of her 1957 M.A. thesis. This book, with its amiable preface by Walter Hooper (recently the subject of accusations of literary fraud, particularly over the authorship of 'Lewis' *The Dark Tower*, by the same Kathryn Lindskoog in her *The C. S. Lewis Hoax* [1988]), is an extremely lively introduction, even if its object is the explication of the ideas in the fiction. Thus we have three main sections, "Spoiled Goodness: Lewis's Concept of Nature," "The Coming of the Lion: Lewis's Concept of God," and "Possible Gods and Goddesses: Lewis's Concept of Man." In the first, for instance, Lindskoog looks at the presentation of nature in all the Narnia books, extending the picture to views expressed by Lewis in such works as *Mere Christianity, The Screwtape Letters, Miracles, Dymer*, and his introduction to D. E. Harding's *The Hierarchy of Heaven and Earth*, and drawing in sources or analogies with the Bible, Norse mythology, Richard Wagner, and Sir James Jeans. Lindskoog's success is in enriching and deepening our understanding of the implications of the Narnia stories, rather than in being reductive: she shows how the books are part of a far larger fabric of imagery and idea. For instance, her picture of Aslan no sooner mentions the symbolizing of Christ as lion in Revelation 5:5 (" 'Weep not; lo, the Lion of the tribe of Judah, the Root of David, has conquered' "), than she goes on to soften the merely allegorical approach by quoting Dorothy Sayers on how God will take a form that suits the natures and the particular worlds of those He creates and redeems (50–51). It is small wonder that Lewis valued this book.

Clyde Kilby's *The Christian World of C. S. Lewis* (1965) is the first account of the totality of Lewis's work; it also provides a useful analysis of the then current research and publication on Lewis. Intended as an introductory overview, it is not immediately concerned with analysis, and thus in the section on the Narnia books, "The Kingdom of Narnia," much of the space is given over to plot summary. This is followed by an account of Lewis's "Christian purpose," of which Kilby believes, "There can be no possible doubt" (136), variously seen in the different books; then Kilby remarks on the vividness of the child and other characters, makes some comparison with Tolkien's idea of "sub-creation," gives some account of the theme of growth, mentions the motifs of joy and longing, and provides a brief list of inconsistencies. While academic criticism may now see Kilby's remarks as rather simplistic or questionable, they do address many of the most immediate issues to strike the minds of readers of the *Chronicles;* and the same can be said of other "straightforward" accounts, which try simply to reflect the plain impact and most evident themes and currents in the stories without looking for their deeper patterns.

We have to wait till 1977 for the next book that gives any substantial place to the *Chronicles of Narnia,* an academic collection of essays, *The Longing for a Form: Essays on the Fiction of C. S. Lewis,* edited by Peter J. Schakel: by then fantasy had achieved a measure of academic, as well as popular, interest. There is a fine essay by Walter Hooper, reworking his "Past Watchful Dragons"; there is a particularly good piece by Charles A. Huttar, "C. S. Lewis's Narnia and the 'Grand Design,' " which points out how the *Chronicles* are both similar to and different from the story in the Bible, and not to be reduced to allegories of our world but rather seen as a "Narnian" bible. There is an essay covering joy and *Sehnsucht* in Lewis's thought and its various forms in the *Chronicles* (interest in Lewis's notion of *Sehnsucht* was already marked, with the publication in particular of Corbin Scott Carnell's *Bright Shadow of Reality: C. S. Lewis and the Feeling Intellect* in 1974). An impressive source study, John D. Cox's "Epistemological Release in *The Silver Chair*" (1977), establishes a clear origin for the underground portion of the story in the episode of Mammon's Cave in Spenser's *The Faerie Queene*, Book 2, and uses this and other sources convincingly to transform our idea of the themes and patterns of this story. But still we are at the level of only occasional new insights into the works.

Chad Walsh's updating in 1979 of his *C. S. Lewis: Apostle to the Skeptics* (1949), in his *The Literary Legacy of C. S. Lewis*, contains a section entitled "The Parallel World of Narnia." He provides insight into the different currents, rational and romantic/imaginative, of Lewis's early literary efforts in "Boxen" and "The Quest for Bleheris" and how they relate to the Narnia books. His discussion, however, focuses on only three of the stories, *The Magician's Nephew*, *The Lion, the Witch and the Wardrobe*, and *The Last Battle*. His account is plot summary, interspersed with commentary. Most of the comments are not new. Like Kilby and Hooper he emphasizes the biblical analogies to the point of making the *Chronicles* an allegory of the Christian story in our world, and even draws up a chart of parallels at one point. It does not trouble him that, for instance, there is no equivalent in Narnia to the Fall of Man that corrupted the whole world.

Far more significant in 1979 was the publication of Peter J. Schakel's *Reading with the Heart: The Way into Narnia*. Schakel's could be called one of the first truly literary approaches to Lewis's work. He reveals certain ruling ideas and narrative rhythms in the stories that give them considerable subtlety of form. For instance, he shows how various modes of magic, from the backless wardrobe to the lion who brings spring to a land of eternal winter to the "Deep Magic" whereby death itself may be reversed, form a leitmotiv running throughout *The Lion, the Witch and the Wardrobe*. He traces the imagery of water in

*The Voyage of the "Dawn Treader"*, and the motifs of belief and disbelief in *Prince Caspian* and of trust and luck in *The Horse and His Boy*. In short, he analyzes the stories to find their deeper patterns. (That is, of course, in harmony with Lewis's own belief that everything apparently random is actually part of a larger pattern.) Another mode of patterning that Schakel traces is one he derived from the ideas on "romance" and the "monomyth" of Northrop Frye, for example in his *The Secular Scripture* (1976). Thus he reads the quest journey in *The Silver Chair* as a pattern of descent and return that is an archetype of literary narrative, and *The Magician's Nephew* and *The Last Battle* as expressions and extensions of a monomythic pattern of movement from winter to summer and back again. So seen, *"The Magician's Nephew* moves from tragedy to comedy and reflects the archetypes of autumn and spring. And *The Last Battle* moves from antiromance to romance, through the archetypes of winter and summer" (98). There are of course some niggles concerning Schakel's approach. The theme of magic could be found just as readily in *The Magician's Nephew*; it is not plain why, with *The Voyage of the "Dawn Treader"* in mind, *The Magician's Nephew* should be singled out as "a story of exploration" (98); and there is a lack of attention to Lewis as an artist at the level of style. But there is no doubt that this book enhances enormously our appreciation of the profundity and literary worth of the Narnia books. And apart from Lindskoog's and Hooper's "background" books, it is the only critical book that is solely devoted to the *Chronicles*.

A good number of books on Lewis's fiction appeared between 1979 and 1981. Thomas Howard's *The Achievement of C. S. Lewis* (1980) covers the *Chronicles* in a section entitled "Narnia: The Forgotten Country," which is actually more about Narnia than about the books themselves. If Narnia is indeed "forgotten," the same cannot be said of Howard himself, whose rather bullying breeziness and affected pseudo-Lewisian personality in the book are all too constantly before us. His primary subject is the status of Narnia as "reality" in its own right, and not as mere allegory of our world. He seeks to explain why the Narnia books are set in an archaic world, contending that it is only through rejection of modernity and return to its mythic roots that

Christianity can be expressed in literature in the modern age. This, given for instance the contemporary and often urban setting of the fantasies of C. S. Lewis's friend Charles Williams, seems simply mistaken. But this book has apparently been well received by critics, and those who are unembarrassed at a critical harlequin turning ecstatic cartwheels within a Christian paddock may find some use for the book.

Evan K. Gibson's *C. S. Lewis, Spinner of Tales: A Guide to His Fiction* (1980) describes Lewis's main characters, and then the plot and significance of each work. Little of novelty emerges from an analysis not much shorter than the whole of Schakel's book, but there is a gentleness and affection of approach that will help the uninitiated into the Narnia books with the assurance that they should enjoy what has immediate appeal (one of Lewis's own principles). Occasional insights enliven the material for the more ambitious reader. Gibson remarks the omnipresence of Lewis as the avuncular narrative persona in the *Chronicles* (134), or the "group" nature of the protagonists as opposed to the single figures in others of Lewis's stories (175), or notes, "If the plot of *The Lion, the Witch and the Wardrobe* is 'Aslan does all', the plot of *Prince Caspian* could be called 'Aslan does nothing' " (162). But the general position is reticent (and founded on the popular "what the author meant" fallacy): "It is easy to find more meaning than Lewis intended" (181).

Donald E. Glover's *C. S. Lewis: The Art of Enchantment* (1981) discusses the style of the Narnia books and provides judgments on their relative value. Glover is concerned with the evolution of both technique and themes in the *Chronicles*. A frequent interest is the structures of individual narratives chapter by chapter. Glover's method yields a large number of insights, almost "happened upon": there is no large-scale novelty of the kind that we find in Schakel, but rather a methodical march through certain areas of interest, from style to plot to theme. Glover tells us how balance is a key to Lewis's method and thus, in contrast to *Perelandra*, chapters in *The Lion, the Witch and the Wardrobe* are of roughly equal length and scenes not lingered over, for the sake of ease of reading for the child (137); or that, "Unlike the Witch who appears unannounced and is then described, we find Lewis first describing Aslan's effect and then showing him in fact"

(141); or of the Witch of Underland in *The Silver Chair*, "her attack upon the children's reason depends upon linguistic inversion, the denial of meaning" (165). He can be critical of Lewis, remarking that the weakness of *The Horse and His Boy* is that the climax of Aslan's appearance comes too early and unannounced (162), or that in *The Magician's Nephew* the juxtaposition of the humble and the great is too much to take: "The admiration which Lewis felt for protected innocence and uncorrupted country virtue is unconvincingly portrayed, and Frank's ennobling is one of the least credible transformations in the *Chronicles*. The book, all in all, seems to plead for too simple and uncomplex a state and is on the whole weaker than other of Lewis's pictures of virtue tested because it is too simple, easy and nice" (178).

The rather inert, repetitive style here is characteristic of Glover, who is not so much precise or analytic in his approach as ruminative and impressionistic. All too often we are left only with his opinion, inadequately argued. Most readers accept Lewis's reticence in describing the more "real" Narnia beyond the stable door in *The Last Battle:* after all, it is by definition beyond our categories. But Glover complains that Lewis is simply shirking the issue: "We are hardly satisfied by being foisted off this way" (186). Glover's less than analytic or "thought-out" approach can lead to critical myopia on his part. For instance, he tells us that description is central to *The Silver Chair*, and we are left to wonder for ourselves where that leaves the emphasis on scenery in *The Voyage of the "Dawn Treader."* Glover's account generally is an uneasy mixture of the obvious and the more penetrating.

The brevity of Brian Murphy's account of the *Chronicles* in his *C. S. Lewis* (1983) does not provide Murphy adequate scope to develop his considerable insights. One point, however, is worth a dozen pages of other critics: "The single great paradoxical truth about this whole series of children's fantasies is that it has all been concerned with one object—the search for the real" (78). Less effective is Joe R. Christopher's 1987 study *C. S. Lewis*, which, largely plot summary, attempts with frequent strain to establish continued source-parallels with Tolkien's *The Lord of the Rings* and *The Silmarillion* throughout; but does very little else with the Narnia books.

In my 1987 text *C. S. Lewis: His Literary Achievement*, the approach to the *Chronicles of Narnia* as literature, so ably begun by Schakel, is continued (as of course it is in this present study). My approach may have its merits, in that it seeks to present and elucidate fresh patterns, structures, and themes in order to reveal the books' dynamism and continual appeal. The approach, however, is a somewhat exclusively literary one, and probably too remorselessly intellectual. I know that there is much in Lewis that loves rigor, clarity, and the complexity of ever-shifting patterns; but there is much scope in him for many more things also.

David Holbrook's *The Skeleton in the Wardrobe: C. S. Lewis's Fantasies: A Phenomenological Study*, appeared in 1991, and gives much space to the *Chronicles*. For those to whom any investigation of an author's supposed sexual proclivities is a fascination, this book will be meat and drink. For Holbrook, Lewis was a repressed sadist with a penchant for whipping, and a mother-fixated adolescent whose children's books are both the expression of his level of development and an arena for the symbolic enactment of fantasies that involve far other things besides Aslan. There is some potential truth here, and such readings have a place where they convince, but in this case the use of evidence is driven all too often by the ax-grinding urge.

Criticism can provide us with information we might otherwise not have gathered from the *Chronicles*, and can at its best enrich our understanding of them. But for the ten million readers who had read them by 1979 and doubtless double that (if diminishing year by year) now, their value is in them alone, unhelped by any review, essay, or critical book. Looked at one way, the *Chronicles of Narnia* have grown through the minds of those sophisticated readers who have written about them; looked at another, that educated growth is an irrelevance, and they live and develop in quite unquantifiable and mysterious modes in the minds and souls of a far wider and less articulate public.

Illustration from *Chronicles of Narnia* by Pauline Baynes, © Pauline Baynes, 1972. Reprinted by permission of Penguin Books.

# A *Reading of the* Chronicles

# 4

## Introduction

How did Lewis come to write fantasies for children? He had little acquaintance with children apart from some wartime evacuee girls who lived at the Kilns, Lewis's house, from 1939 to 1942. There is no doubt that like George MacDonald, one of his most powerful literary and spiritual influences, he valued the childlike as he saw it: in his *Perelandra* (1943) he celebrates the innocence of a naked green lady in a planetary paradise. But of course there is a difference between the childlike and the child, and the depiction of the one and the other involves quite different skills. Lewis in his fiction recreated something of his own childhood with his brother Warnie, added to by his enthusiastic reading of George MacDonald, Kenneth Grahame, Edith Nesbit, John Masefield, and Arthur Ransome. Though his child characters often sound dated, many of them are remarkably vivid and memorable, not least because Lewis had an uncanny ability to see things through their imagined minds—one thinks of Lucy Pevensie, of the snobbish Eustace Scrubb, the impulsive Jill Pole, the overhumble Shasta, the too-curious Digory Kirke.

A. N. Wilson in his biography of Lewis has claimed, if without any *clear* evidence, that Lewis was probably driven to write such fiction after the celebrated worsting of his *Miracles* by the philosopher Elizabeth Anscombe at a meeting of the Oxford Socratic Club in early 1948. Wilson says that this had a quite shattering effect on Lewis, turning him away from direct Christian apologetics and back to a conversation he had had with Tolkien about the far greater potency of myth over argument—this of course on the assumption that Lewis's primary object was still to "affect" and "convert" a readership. At the same time, Wilson points to an escapist impulse in Lewis that he says could only have been heightened by his felt humiliation by Anscombe. In a fictional world, his vision would be unassailable. What is certainly true is that Lewis was under considerable domestic strain in the period 1948–51. Mrs. Moore, to whom for decades he had acted as house-keeper, nurse, and perhaps (earlier) even lover went into senile decline and became so demanding that the strain was too much for Lewis; he became ill and was admitted for a time into a nursing home. Mrs. Moore herself was eventually transferred to a rest home but lingered till 1951, all the time demanding visits by Lewis, from which he would return emotionally drained. Furthermore, Lewis's long friendship with Tolkien was dying, largely through emerging differences over religion (Tolkien was a firm Roman Catholic); and his brother, to whom he might have turned for help, was more often than not incapacitated by drink. Feeling himself increasingly alone, what better consolation, Wilson argues, than to create a new world in which friendships are made and the world perpetually renewed by the immediate breath of a divine lion?[1] (Lewis, we may remark, recalled "having a good many dreams of lions about that time."[2]) Certainly we must wonder at the sheer speed with which the books were written. Lewis claimed he wrote them all within one year, but the evidence seems to show that the first five were completed between late 1948 and early 1951, and the last two by 1953.[3] The series' name, the *Chronicles of Narnia*, was suggested to Lewis by his friend Roger Lancelyn Green, following *The Chronicles of Pantouflia* of Andrew Lang.[4]

Weight must also be given to the "ideological" sources of the books, even if Lewis did not say what these were until after they were written. He was asked how the stories came to be, why he wrote in the fairy-tale form, and whether he was seeking to propagate Christian truth in disguised form. To the last question he produced ambiguous response. At times he agreed that he was trying to steal past the "watchful dragons" of a public immune to overt Christian teaching and stained-glass imagery, by setting his stories in a strange world where his readers would be suddenly surprised into awareness of how, say, the sacrifice of Aslan the lion and its subsequent resurrection in *The Lion, the Witch and the Wardrobe* parallels the story of Christ. Yet Lewis could also argue that what was primary in his stories was not any Christian message but an image. In the essay "Sometimes Fairy Stories May Say Best What's to Be Said" (1956) he declared, "Everything began with images; a faun carrying an umbrella, a queen on a sledge, a magnificent lion. At first there wasn't even anything Christian about them; that element pushed itself in of its own accord."[5] And beyond this, he could maintain that even the patterns of suggestive spiritual significance that *did* emerge in his stories were not allegories of events in the world, but were applicable only to the "fantastic" worlds in which they were set. His hero, Ransom, on the planet Perelandra is brought to realize that he cannot make comparisons between the temptation of the lady in that paradise and the temptation of Eve in Eden, because, "This chapter, this page, this very sentence, in the cosmic story was utterly and eternally itself; no other passage that had occurred or ever would occur could be substituted for it."[6] So we have, variously, Lewis the artist primarily concerned with images and their setting in narratives, Lewis the covert Christian, and Lewis the explorer of divine narratives in other worlds. The dominance of one or the other will naturally vary from book to book.

There was also for Lewis a certain literary value in writing for children (by which he meant the childlike) and, in particular, in choosing the fairy tale as the form in which to write. Of course the Narnia books are in no way like fairy tales in any conventional sense: no "once upon a time" here, no evil stepmothers, wishes or tests in triplicate, princesses or kingdoms to be won. There is a strange world, Narnia, but it is visited in very specific modern times from our world. There may have been a wicked witch in fairy tale (beautiful too, as in "Snow White"), but there never was a divine lion, nor a journey by ship to the uttermost east, nor the making and the destruction of a world; and nothing in fairy tale could prepare us for a Marsh-wiggle. However, Lewis saw the books as following certain basic characteristics of the fairy tale, which emerged in the process of composition. Starting with images as he claimed to do, the next thing was to find a form that suited them. "As these images sorted themselves into events (i.e. became a story) they seemed to demand no love interest and no close psychology. But the Form which excludes these things is the fairy tale. And the moment I thought of that I fell in love with the Form itself: its brevity, its severe restraints on description, its flexible traditionalism, its inflexible hostility to all analysis, digression, reflections and 'gas.' "[7]

What is at the foundation of this is an emphasis on narrative itself. It is true that we have some very vivid characters in the Narnia books. But there is, as Lewis says (and here there is strong contrast with what he called "a modern fairy-tale for grown-ups," his *That Hideous Strength* (1945)), very little in the way of speculation, thought, contemplation, even rest. One will not find here the lengthy descriptions of landscape that we see in *Out of the Silent Planet* and *Perelandra*; nor the analyses of the spirit that run throughout *The Great Divorce* and *Till We Have Faces*. Here things are always revealed and done through plain story. Narnia is progressively realized through the adventures of the children as first they enter it and then begin to take an increasing part in its history. In the Narnia books a fascination Lewis had all his life with "story" is most purely realized. Indeed, he actually claimed in one of his essays that the element of story in fantasy, that sequence of causality linking the images and characters into one possible molecular chain, had a unique capacity to embody a sense of the numinous. Lewis spoke of story writing as an endeavor to catch an elusive "something," like a bird, in a net of events:

> In life and art both, as it seems to me, we are always trying to catch in our net of successive moments something that is not successive. Whether in real life there is any doctor who can teach us how to do it, so that at last either the meshes will become fine enough to hold the bird, or we be so changed that we can throw our nets away and follow the bird to its own country, is not a question for this essay. But I think it is sometimes done—or very, very nearly done—in stories. I believe the effort to be well worth making.[8]

And in a sense the whole history of Narnia that we have in the seven books of the *Chronicles* could be called one attempt to catch that elusive bird (perhaps here emblematized in the intermittent presence of Aslan) until like a net, Narnia itself is "thrown away" and the children pass beyond it to new and more real Narnias, and beyond that to countries of which no tongue can speak and in which they begin "Chapter One of the Great Story, which no one on earth has read: which goes on for ever: in which every chapter is better than the one before."

# 5

## The Lion, the Witch and the Wardrobe

*The Lion, the Witch and the Wardrobe*, probably the best known of the Narnia books, stands alone perhaps more than any other book of the *Chronicles*. It is true that several of the other stories are "finished" in the sense of being self-contained: a rightful king or prince is restored in *Prince Caspian*, *The Silver Chair*, and *The Horse and His Boy*; a voyage to the end of the world is completed in *The Voyage of the "Dawn Treader."* Yet we know that these narratives are excerpts from the history of Narnia, with a before and after, where the first book is our first account of the country. (We know too that Lewis originally wrote it with no thought to a sequel.[1]) Lewis struck in *The Lion, the Witch and the Wardrobe* a blend of fantasy and the everyday that he was not again to match. The book is an extraordinary mixture of diverse things, from a lion who is a Narnian Christ to a witch out of fairy tale, from a Father Christmas out of myth to a female beaver with a sewing machine drawn from Beatrix Potter, from a society of articulate beasts and animate trees to a group of strongly characterized children partly derived from Edith Nesbit. This is the only book in which the children themselves become kings and queens of Narnia. In all the others they are relative outsiders, and in all but *The Magician's*

*Nephew* the rulers of Narnia come from within the fantastic realm. This separation adds to the sense of a Narnia that goes on without them. The "proximity" of the children to Narnia in *The Lion*, their close involvement in its transformation from deathly winter to the spring of new life, gives that book a special poignancy: the children do not come so close to the innocence of a fantastic world again, not even in *The Magician's Nephew*, where Narnia is created by Aslan. In *The Voyage of the "Dawn Treader,"* the image of spiritual longing realized in the risen life of Aslan, and the victory and enthronement of the children as Sons of Adam and Daughters of Eve, is found only by going out of the world, by journeying across the seas to its end and beyond: what was "immanent" in *The Lion* is there found only by a process of transcendence. Narnia in *The Lion* is increasingly and uniquely shot through with holiness, embodied in the coming and eventual victory of Aslan. In the later books it is a much more secular world, with Aslan's presence more limited. *The Lion* seems to contain a pattern of spiritual renewal sufficient to itself: the winter of the White Witch is turned to spring, the cold laws of the Stone Table are transcended by the grace of Aslan's sacrifice, the sin of man is washed away in the restoration of Adam and Eve's lineage to their rightful thrones, the devil in the shape of the White Witch is finally slain, the paradise that was lost is regained. The whole seems to encapsulate something of the primal rhythm of Christian history, within the idiom of another world.

Lewis's method of introducing us to the realm of Narnia is, per- haps naturally, much more gradual in *The Lion* than in the later books, where the children are suddenly whisked away from a railway station where they are waiting to go their several ways to boarding school (*Prince Caspian*), or fall into a picture of an ancient sailing ship (*The Voyage of the "Dawn Treader"*), or are transported to Narnia via their deaths in a railway crash (*The Last Battle*). *The Lion, the Witch and the Wardrobe* portrays the gradual joining of two worlds. The emphasis in this novel, as in *The Magician's Nephew* and *The Last Battle*, which respectively describe the creation and eventual "uncre- ation" of Narnia, is on the permeability of Narnia (there through its fragility of being, here as part of a divine plan): it is entered, variously, by the children (on three different occasions), by Father Christmas, and by Aslan himself. It is of course a place that needs stimulus from the outside if it is to regain life at all, for it is a world frozen to perpetual winter by an evil witch, and nothing will change so long as she and her ice have power over it. But more than this, the book describes a gradual *incarnating:* not only Aslan's actions but the children's presence, long prophesied, in making themselves part of this world, will overthrow the witch and restore Narnia to its true nature.

For the moment let us deal with the first point, the gradualness of the approach. First the children are withdrawn from society by being sent away from the London air raids in wartime to their uncle's house in the remote country, "ten miles from the nearest railway station and two miles from the nearest post office" (9). This uncle is odd-looking; he has so much white hair that it "grew over most of his face as well as on his head" (9). The servants of the house are mentioned only to be dismissed as of no consequence to the story. The children are left free to do as they wish. All the time, identity and boundaries are melting away. The house is vast and uncharted. The world outside it seems a wilderness of mountains and woods, with the possibility of eagles, stags, and hawks among them, as well as the more domestic badgers, foxes, and rabbits (10). There is a hint here of likeness to the landscape of the world the children are to enter.

The discovery of Narnia, too, is gradual. One rainy day the children set out to explore the house, and one of them, Lucy (from *lux* meaning "light" or "perception"), investigates the inside of an old wardrobe in an otherwise empty room. It is a casual-seeming occurrence that turns to something quite other. Beyond one line of fur coats in the wardrobe Lucy finds another, and then as she pushes through that and feels the ground begin to crunch under her feet, fur turns to fir and she finds herself in a pine forest with the snow falling. The gradualism here is a marvelous tapering of everyday world into fantastic realm.

Once in this strange new world, Lucy meets a faun, Mr. Tumnus, in the forest, and it emerges, as she takes tea with him in his home, that he is a spy for the wicked White Witch. Having remorsefully confessed this, he ushers Lucy back through the wardrobe into her own world. Lucy is amazed to find that no time has passed in her absence—which could make her experience seem a dream. She tells the others of her adventure but they do not believe her, least of all the scoffing Edmund; and the wardrobe when examined by the children is now obstinately nothing but a wardrobe. Aslan's purposes transcend human wish and will. After some days, during a game of hide-and-seek on another wet day, Lucy has hidden in the wardrobe and Edmund pursues her there, only to find himself in Narnia. He then meets the White Witch herself, and she, mindful of the menace to her if the prophecy should come true and four humans become rightful kings and queens of Narnia, bribes Edmund to bring his brother and sisters to her castle. Edmund finds Lucy on his way back to the wardrobe in the Narnian wood (she has been with Mr. Tumnus again), but when they return to their uncle's house and Lucy looks to Edmund for support, he tells the others that he has only been humoring Lucy's delusion. The next move occurs one day when all four children are trying to escape a group of visitors who are being given a tour through the house. They are eventually driven to the room with the wardrobe and through the wardrobe itself into Narnia. Now *all* believe, and what is believed *in* has shifted from an indefinite place to another world in which they are set. First one, then two, then four children have entered Narnia.

Once there, there are further gradations. At first visitors, the children are brought to realize that they are in part the focus of the hopes of the Narnian creatures. What seemed accident is part of a larger pattern, if they will play their part, and if Aslan comes to help. Initially guests of the Beavers, the three children (Edmund having sneaked away to the witch) are soon active agents in the cause of Narnia. And what Narnia is and means continually deepens. At first perhaps a fairy-tale world, it does not stop being that while also being a landscape of the spirit frozen in primal sin; and the witch, who seems something straight out of Hans Christian Andersen, retains something of this fairy-tale "lightness" while at the same time becoming an agent of ultimate evil, daughter of Lilith and the giants, and ancient enemy of Aslan. Then, too, we have what seem to be layers of magic, with the witch's evil wand that turns creatures to stone at one level, and the "Deep Magic" by which Aslan may through sacrificial death rise again, at quite another. Aslan himself is lion and much more than lion. As for the children, they do not till the end stop being themselves even when accomplishing heroic deeds. The Peter who slays Maugrim, the witch's great wolf, is still a frightened but resolute boy, and the Edmund who, reformed, hinders the witch from final victory in the battle by breaking her wand, is awarded plaudits which make him at once heroic and the brightest boy in the class.

But by this point the children are very "far in" (to use one of Lewis's favorite phrases). Just as the story has taken them to a world inside a wardrobe inside a room in a house within the heart of beleaguered England, so they have penetrated to the center of Narnia and in the end become its cynosures, as they sit dispensing justice and largess on the four thrones at the castle of Cair Paravel. They are the sovereign human element long missing from the hierarchy of rational or "Talking Beasts" of Narnia, and in that sense they belong most fully to that world. At that point things have changed: they are no longer children but young adults, they have forgotten their own world, and they speak the elevated language of medieval romance. That loss of former self, and the length of sojourn in Narnia, is found with no other of the children of the *Chronicles*: Lewis has steadily moved the children away from their old selves and understandings until they become wholly part of another world. Even the style that describes them has changed: "And they entered into friendship and alliance with countries beyond the sea and paid them visits of state and received visits of state from them. And they themselves grew and changed as the years passed over them" (166); "So they lived in great joy and if ever they remembered their life in this world it was only as one remembers a dream" (167). And then having accomplished this, Lewis briskly returns the children to their own world through their pursuit of a white stag that leads them to a thicket wherein is the wardrobe; through which they return to England, abruptly restored to child form and their present-day clothes, having been absent, by the time of this world, for not one moment. This perhaps serves as an exercise in humility and a reminder that nothing that is mortal is permanent (a point to be made much more openly concerning Narnia itself in *The Last Battle*).

To some extent what is portrayed in this process is a form of spiritual development on the part of the children. They are asked to develop out of an old awareness into a new. They must show faith, trust, compassion, perception, and courage in transforming Narnia. It may be mistaken to see what happens too much from Narnia's point of view, with the children its promised saviors. It might be better to recall also that Lewis was steeped in allegory, and particularly in Spenser's *The Faerie Queene*, in which the landscape of Fairy Land is that of the soul. Narnia is, in one sense at least, a country within a wardrobe; a wardrobe seems an appropriate conveyance to Narnia, as it is a place for different clothes. If, too, we were to think of the children not just as four individuals, but also potentially as four parts of the one spirit, we might not always be wide of the mark. When the children first see Mr. Beaver surreptitiously beckoning to them from among the Narnian trees, the following exchange ensues:

> "It wants us to go to it," said Susan, "and it is warning us not to make a noise."
> "I know," said Peter. "The question is, are we to go to it or not? What do you think, Lu?"
> "I think it's a nice beaver," said Lucy.
> "Yes, but how do we *know*?" said Edmund.
> "Shan't we have to risk it?" said Susan. "I mean, it's no good just standing here and I feel I want some dinner." (62)

It is possible to see Susan as "the body" here, simply observing and registering physical needs, with Peter as "reason," Lucy as the enlightened soul, and Edmund as the evil side of the self. Such a reading is certainly too stark, and the characters do play other roles elsewhere in the narrative. But the story as a whole can be seen as a spiritual journey through a landscape of the soul, from the frost of original sin to the flowers of the redeemed spirit; one in which the kingship and queenship reached at the end, and the completion of the hierarchy of creation in Narnia by the humans, suggest the integration and potential perfection of the soul in Christ. Such a reading might explain why in this book, the children are frequently isolated from one another (just as, say, Una and Redcrosse are divided in the first book of *The Faerie*

*Queene*): Lucy alone, then Edmund alone, then Edmund away from the other three, then the girls absent from their brothers, and finally all four united. It is as though the spirit is broken up to be reconstituted. This reading at the very least shows how no single understanding of Narnia or the characters in it is adequate—there are multiple possibilities.

Either way, literally or allegorically, what is portrayed in *The Lion, the Witch and the Wardrobe* is growth away from the old self. Growth out of death is a theme central to the book, as Aslan dies to bring new life and winter turns to spring: that is the allegorical and anagogical level of the book (to use Dante's terms), where with the children the development is at the moral or tropological level. The antitype here is of course the witch. She is concerned only with maintaining her power over Narnia. She does nothing with it, exists for no other reason than to keep it (in contrast to the multiple activities of the children when they are kings and queens of Narnia). And Narnia expresses the nature of her spirit: frozen, uniform, static. For all life that thinks to exist independently of her will she has one answer: turn it to stone. Her castle seems to have nothing in it, and she herself in the end *is* nothing. That was the course Edmund would have gone. Drawn to her by his own self-conceit (where Lucy meets Mr. Tumnus, he "happens" upon the witch), he is tempted to bring his brother and sisters into her power to satisfy his appetites in the form of the Turkish Delight she offers him.

Where those whose allegiance is to the witch take, those whose allegiance is to Aslan give. The children are the long-awaited gift to Narnia. Aslan is a gift beyond telling, his coming turning winter to spring. He gives his life for Edmund's. Even Narnia itself, as a place of recovered innocence, is a gift of high adventure to the children. Right at the center of the narrative, not the anomaly he has sometimes been seen,[2] is the arrival of Father Christmas, with a sackful of gifts for everyone. And *The Lion, the Witch and the Wardrobe* as a whole is a "box of delights" full for the reader of the most wonderful creatures and events, which become still richer as one "opens" them. The book, as a progressive revelation of Aslan's nature and of the deepest potential of the children, is like a gift gradually arrived at.

## The Lion, the Witch and the Wardrobe

The narrowness of the self is "answered" in the character of the narrative of the book. Its title, *The Lion, the Witch and the Wardrobe*, suggests its creation out of at least three separate acts of the imagination. But all come together to make a pattern long foreseen: each "separate" item is part of a larger unity. So it is with the plot itself, which is really a series of "microplots." At first there is the issue of whether or not Narnia is real. Then there is the plan of the witch to seize the children and their escape from her. With Aslan's arrival, and spring's, the witch seems defeated, especially when Edmund is rescued from death at her hands. But then there is a new plot begun by her claim to Edmund's life through an old law that makes traitors forfeit to her. The later stages of conflict with the witch involve two plots: in one Peter, Edmund, and the Narnians fight her and her forces, while in the other Aslan breathes new life into the Narnians who were made statues at the witch's castle so that they may come to the aid of the others. All these little plots amalgamate to bring about the realization of the grand design, like little selves cooperating with others. And this idea of cooperation, of society, is central. The children themselves are constituents of Narnian society, to which we are progressively introduced throughout. This particular use of microplots is unique to *The Lion, the Witch and the Wardrobe*. Other books (apart from *The Magician's Nephew*) have a much more clear-cut quest or objective from the outset, but here a series of apparently local and unconnected doings together provide the key to unlock Narnia. In a sense, too, these isolated doings might in some cases suggest the benightedness of the soul amid evil: conditions under the witch in Narnia are such that incoherence is inevitable. Then the nighttime setting of many of the scenes in Narnia is also significant; and that Father Christmas arrives, Aslan rises again, and final victory over the witch is won in the morning.

Other features of the book seem to belong to this rejection of narrowness. For one thing, there is, as already partly seen, the theme of growing and of expansion. Growth is inherent in the story itself, which from apparently small beginnings involving a girl and a faun becomes an epic on which the fate of an entire world depends. Narnia is wakened from its sleep, the talking animals from their hiding-places, the spellbound creatures from stone, Aslan from death itself. The adventure begins through a "narrow" wardrobe that turns out to open onto a whole world. Inside Narnia the perspective gradually expands. At first the omnipresence of the snow makes the adventures relatively local: Mr. Tumnus here, the Beavers there, the White Witch beyond. Gradually creatures congregate, and we begin to get a sense of Narnia as a whole and of the issues at stake. The Stone Table commands a view of all Narnia. Cair Paravel, the ultimate destination of the children, is in an open place by the shore of a sea that stretches to the world's end. The witch's castle however, is set in a hollow among hills, shut in on itself. She lives alone, but for the children the whole story involves an increase of friends: they themselves become the centers of a whole society.

We might extrapolate from the way that the White Witch has converted Narnia to a mirror image of herself in the form of one monotonous dead white, the mode by which Lewis refuses to let us settle to one view of a thing. Throughout, the children continually have their assumptions displaced. Mr. Tumnus is not just the jolly domestic host he appears to be; the wardrobe is more than a wardrobe; Narnia is not an illusion; Edmund is not rewarded by the witch; Edmund's rescue from the witch is not final; Aslan is not dead, but even more alive than before; they who were kings and queens of Narnia are in an instant returned to being modern children. Reality is not to be appropriated; its richness and depth elude ready absorption by mind. Our idea of Narnia is continually altered: at first apparently a little "play" world, it becomes more threatening with the witch, more metaphysical with Aslan, more holy in its ultimate foundation through Aslan's journey. Even then we are not to know the true and further realities until the afterworlds of *The Last Battle* are revealed, and Narnia upon Narnia lead us "farther up and farther in." Nothing is "mere": Lewis chose children as heroic protagonists to demonstrate that fact.

The object of the witch is to reduce all things to one dead level, to draw them back into herself. But the object of the story is in part to show how different, how "other" from one another things can be. To our minds Narnia may suggest the world of Andersen's "Snow

Queen," of Kenneth Grahame or of traditional Christmas, but such a stereotype is swiftly dispelled as we find that this is a world in which the struggle between good and evil is between God and the devil. And if we then proceed to see similarities between Aslan's sacrifice and that of Christ in our world, we at once see that they are also quite different. Aslan is a lion in another world called Narnia. His voluntary death as a substitute for Edmund is not the same as Christ's less-chosen Crucifixion, nor His effective death on behalf of all men. Even the special sordid intimacy of Aslan's stabbing by the witch is quite different from Christ's more solitary and drawn-out bodily pain on the cross. Nor is it Aslan alone who saves Narnia: he does that through the mortal agency of the children and the Narnians themselves. The Deep Magic ordained by the "Emperor," whereby all traitors are forfeit to the witch or else all Narnia will be destroyed, is quite different in form from the "magic" that binds our world. Of course there are similarities. The process whereby Aslan dies only to rise again transfigured, is like Christ's death and resurrection. The breaking of the great Stone Table on which he is sacrificed is perhaps like the breaking of the power of the grave: as he tells the children, the witch did not know the "Deeper Magic" that "when a willing victim who had committed no treachery was killed in a traitor's stead, the Table would crack and Death itself would start working backwards" (148). In terms of ultimate metaphysics, this is what Christ's death brought about in our world: though in Narnia the idea of death working backward has much more immediate and absolute import, in the sense that the deathlike winter of the witch's power over Narnia is now destroyed, and with the children enthroned Narnia will for the time become a recovered paradise. The basic pattern of the magic that Aslan enacts, because it is a spiritual rhythm based on divine reality, will be the same in all worlds; but in all worlds it will also be uniquely manifested.

*The Lion, the Witch and the Wardrobe*, then, dramatizes the difference between good and evil. There is more attention to the good, because it is more real. The witch as yet has no name, nor has her dwarf; she and her agents are present much less than the Narnians, Aslan, and the children. Where she is separate from Narnia, the children become progressively more involved, "farther in." She can only reduce things—Narnia to stasis, the rational creatures of Narnia to stone, Aslan to a shorn cat—even herself, at Edmund's rescue, to a mere formless boulder. In opposition to her the book is full of selves and "things." In no other of the Narnia books are the children so distinguished from one another: the impetuous, loving and perceptive Lucy, the rather more stolid and self-regarding Susan, the cynical and jealous Edmund, the rational and brave Peter. In themselves they are complex, a varying compound of good and evil that the witch can never be; and as a group they form a multiple nature. Further, they all change and develop through the narrative. Then there is the variety of creatures in Narnia, and of the objects that surround them. There are a faun, a pair of beavers, Father Christmas, a great lion who is more than lion, and a group of modern children. The variety is heightened by juxtapositions—fur coats and fir trees, a lamppost in a wood, a faun with an umbrella, a female beaver with a sewing machine. The book conveys a gradual increase of population—first one faun, then two beavers, then a party of Narnians at a table; by the time the children and the beavers reach the hill of the Stone Table where a pavilion is pitched, the pace of creation seems suddenly to leap, as they find Aslan surrounded by a whole group of Narnians as though they had been begotten by him—which, since he has released them from the Narnian winter, is in part true. Still more it is true later when he recreates more of the Narnians out of the stone to which the witch has turned them by the even more deadly winter of her wand. For Aslan death "is only more life."[3] Everything that is good grows, and grows still more like its true nature.

At the center is Aslan. We see the witch early, but he is long heralded before his appearance. When first we see him the first words are, "Aslan stood." He is the creator, not the created; he is supreme being, *Yahweh*, "I am" (Exodus 3:14), to the witch's negativity. He radiates being to all about him. In him oppositions are not at war, as in most mortals, but are brought into energetic unity: he is both god and lion, both lovable and fearful. "People who have not been in Narnia sometimes think that a thing cannot be good and terrible at the same time. If the children had ever thought so, they were cured of it now. For when they tried to look at Aslan's face they just caught a glimpse of the golden mane and the great, royal, solemn, overwhelming eyes; and then they found they couldn't look at him and went all trembly" (117). In the wake of the shame and humiliation of his death he can still play with the children in a romp at which "whether it was more like playing with a thunderstorm or playing with a kitten Lucy could never make up her mind" (148–49).

• • •

The theme of growth and expansion that we have seen in this story is one that will be found throughout the *Chronicles of Narnia;* the enemy will always be that which shuts in, isolates, or immobilizes. Every story will have a variation on the idea of no time at all passing in our world while the children have their adventures in Narnia, so that they return to waiting at a railway station, looking at a picture in a bedroom, or to a school where they are being pursued by bullies, at exactly the moment they left. Every book will show a gradual increase in society, from more or less isolated figures at the start, to gathering groups and then often meetings with whole peoples. Space, too, will grow, just as in *The Lion* a wardrobe opened into a forest, and that forest was found to be part of a whole country, and that country of a world. . . . There will be a similar process in *Prince Caspian*. In *The Voyage of the "Dawn Treader"* a picture of a ship will turn into an actual ship on a wide ocean, and a voyage to the east will extend through realm after realm until it reaches the truest realm of all. In *The Silver Chair* we will begin to explore the lands to the west of Narnia. In *The Horse and His Boy* we will be outside Narnia, in the land of Calormen, traveling back. In *The Magician's Nephew* we will enter three different worlds by magic. And in *The Last Battle* the Narnia we know will give way to larger and ever more real Narnias beyond it. And all this enlargement will be preparing us for the final journey to Aslan's country at the end of *The Last Battle*, a place of living paradox where the smaller contains the greater, where true progression is found where there is no time, where to go "farther up and farther in" is to go farther out, and where one's true identity exists beyond the loss of self in death. Meanwhile, throughout, the *Chronicles of Narnia* will be telling

# 6

## *Prince Caspian*

The story of *Prince Caspian* is quite similar in broad outline to that of *The Lion, the Witch and the Wardrobe*. The Pevensie children—Peter, Susan, Edmund, and Lucy—return to Narnia to help the rightful King Caspian overthrow a usurper, his uncle Miraz. In this Narnia the Talking Beasts, if they have not lost their powers of speech, have gone underground, and the trees have to be awakened. Aslan appears to guide the children through Narnia to meet with Caspian.

But this similarity does serve to throw the contrasts of the two stories into relief. This is not the Narnia of the White Witch's time or near it, but a Narnia a thousand years beyond that, where the memory of the children as High Kings and Queens has sunk to a legend known only to the Old, or indigenous, Narnians. Down a line of kings from Caspian I the Conqueror, Narnia has been ruled by people from the neighboring country of Telmar. The idea of a single and mythically self-contained world is gone: now it is one among other realms. The apotheosis that ended *The Lion, the Witch and the Wardrobe* has become a prelude to history. Narnia is here a much more secular world. Miraz is a selfish and greedy man, though not evil itself, as was the witch. The issues are more political and dynastic. Miraz was prepared to let Caspian reign after him, until his queen bore him a son. With that event the prince must flee for his life. Aslan's part in the story is more as a sustainer of Caspian's struggle than as an agent of change. He helps the children reach Caspian and his army, and "wakens" first thousands of dryads, hamadryads, and sylvans to assist Caspian, and then sends a battalion of awakened Narnian trees to smash Miraz's army; later he helps restore Narnia to its wild self, and gives the Telmarines the choice of staying in Narnia or leaving. His presence serves more as a *reminder* of the ultimate foundations of the Narnian world than as its central feature, as it was in *The Lion, the Witch and the Wardrobe*. In a sense—but only in a sense—all "supernatural" intervention is unnecessary in this world: it was not *essential* that the Old Narnians be weaker in power than the army of Miraz, and thus need Aslan's help in the way that it was essential to have four Sons of Adam and Daughters of Eve enter Narnia to over-throw the witch and fulfill the prophecy, or for Aslan to reverse the power of death. (Still less, we may remark, are the children in *The Voyage of the "Dawn Treader"* essential to the success of the quest: it may be that this is a way of showing that one's value need not be determined solely by one's use.) It is Peter rather than Caspian who fights with Miraz, probably because Lewis is reluctant to have Caspian fight with his own uncle, who in the past had sometimes meant well enough, according to his limited lights. If we recall Lewis's love of Spenser's *The Faerie Queene*, this is the much more secular book 2 concerning a Guyon, where *The Lion* is more like the holy and Christian book 1 (in which a lion also gives its life to save someone).

This said, the repetition of the basic narrative of *The Lion, the Witch and the Wardrobe* in *Prince Caspian* does admit to some weak-ness of inspiration. The same basic pattern is followed in the latter book as the former—a denatured Narnia, its peoples in hiding, is brought awake to overthrow the tyranny that has gripped it. There are also more local similarities, such as the children arriving just in time to save Caspian and his army, just as Aslan and the awakened stone creatures do for Peter and the Narnians in their fight with the White Witch in the earlier book; Peter fighting the witch is echoed in his contest with Miraz; and *Prince Caspian* culminates, as did *The*

*Lion*, in the enthronement of a rightful ruler, and in feasting. There is an occasion where Lucy meets Aslan by night and romps with him in a clear repetition of the frolic after the resurrection in *The Lion*; and the girls ride on Aslan's back to the town of Beruna in *Prince Caspian* just as they rode to the witch's castle in *The Lion*. Nor do many episodes strike us with quite the vividness they had in *The Lion*. The children's sudden transportation to Narnia and sojourn on the island that holds the ruin of Cair Paravel is quite vivid, particularly in the way that they gradually grasp where they are; but the account of the journey across Narnia is slightly blurred, and still more uncertain is Aslan's How or the country about it. The various woodland deities— Bacchus, the Maenads, even the trees themselves in their attack on Miraz's army—are rather sketchy, the trees far more so than Tolkien's Ents from which they are derived. Lewis's imagination has not caught fire to the same degree that it did in *The Lion*, nor with the same novelty. And yet—perhaps out of an unconscious sense of the need for it—he is often in *Prince Caspian* at pains to try to convey personality and individuality, whether through the labored account of how the dwarf Trumpkin is forced to eat his words about mere children being not quite what he expected of High Kings and Queens; or of the Bulgy Bear who keeps forfeiting his dignity by putting his paws in his mouth; or of the mouse Reepicheep and his humiliation at the loss of his tail in battle. There is not quite the pressure behind his narrative that there was in *The Lion*: and the ultimate reason may be that the book is simply an adventure so far as the Pevensie children are concerned— following a trail, avoiding the arrows of sentries, being on the winning side of a battle and then going on a triumphant progress with the whole diversity of the life of Narnia, and with Aslan. As Peter says at the end, "Well! . . . We *have* had a time." There is a definite sense, for all the themes and significance that there are in the book, that, so far as the narrative goes, this has been largely a play world, a relaxation and recreation compared to *The Lion*.

Some of these are hard statements: and while the book may not be always powerful or convincing, it is well organized. One of the unifying ideas might be called "appropriation." A similar idea in *The Lion* is the motif of undermining assumptions. The children are themselves rarely guilty of appropriation, but what we find from the outset is a Narnia that is no longer theirs. Now it is not even in their "time": a millennium has passed since their rule and the rightful human king has no connection with them. They are still important—though not *vitally* so—to Caspian's success: they are rather more "welcome extra help" than the essential key to Narnia's salvation. Their former palace is a ruin, its location no longer a promontory but an island. When they discover its true nature, it is to realize more fully how they do not belong as they did. They find an old chess-piece they once used; they realize that the fruit trees that grow up to the wall are the descendants of the orchard long ago planted in their reign; they break their way through a wall of ivy into their ancient treasure chamber. Wherever they go it is, "Do you remember?"; but now it is mere memory, not to be revived. Except for one thing: the old gifts of Father Christmas, of sword and shield, bow and health-giving phial, which are to be used on their adventure. And then of course as they travel through Narnia, even its landscape has changed, and they spend much time trying to cross a hitherto unknown gorge; and the site of the former Stone Table where they meet Caspian is now a hill thrown up over the table, called Aslan's How. The children, while honored guests and friends in need, have no longer a central part to play in Narnia's history. Their task is to put someone from within the Narnian world on its throne, no longer to reign themselves. This displacement is seen in the way that the fourth to seventh chapters of the book are told from the point of view of Caspian rather than of the children: even if it is Trumpkin the dwarf who is telling the children the history of Caspian, it is not told in his idiom, and the book thus early on has two centers of consciousness.

Displacement seems the motif here. The children are abruptly displaced, at the control of others, from the railway station to Narnia. Within Narnia they are in a sense anachronisms: and one might say that the interruption in the narrative while Trumpkin brings them up-to-date with events is a parallel to the way they themselves have mentally to adjust over the one-thousand-year interruption between their first time in Narnia and now. We find this idea of displacement in the changes in Narnian geography (which make Narnia in fact another place); in the way the Old Narnians have been conquered by the invading Telmarines; in the rightful King Caspian's flight from court into exile; even in the very fact that when the children are summoned back to Narnia by Caspian's blowing of Susan's horn, they do not come to Aslan's How where he is, but to distant Cair Paravel, so that they are effectively "displaced" from him and must make a journey to meet him. This theme of displacement is one we will find occurring throughout the *Chronicles:* it is a means always of shaking loose the self from settled assumptions, of undercutting human appropriations of reality.

To return briefly now to the idea of "appropriation" in relation to the rest of the book. The Telmarines invaded and seized Narnia. His uncle Miraz has usurped the throne of the "rightful Telmarine King Caspian the Tenth." Both of these must be "displaced": Miraz must be deposed and Caspian enthroned in his stead; and the Telmarines must be given the choice of returning to their own world, or of becoming true Narnians with all the life of Narnia that will be restored to its own. The Narnia that has been seized and "civilized" into bridges, roads, and towns must be released to find its own equilibrium once more: the river god asks to be freed from his chains, and is so by the destruction of the bridge over the Beruna by the disjointing power of Bacchus and his ivy. Equally, set ideas are undermined, as Trumpkin the dwarf must be brought to realize that Peter, Edmund, Susan, and Lucy are not to be dismissed as mere children, but are in fact the High Kings and Queens in the guise of children. Perhaps certain features of the new geography of Narnia suggest this: the land that cuts the children off from the mainland, the gorge that checks their progress, suggest bars to the mind's dominance over the world; and the network of tunnels beneath the serene appearance of the hill, Aslan's How, may again symbolize the deeper and more complex world beneath simple views of reality.

The dominant mood of the book is interrogative. What has so suddenly brought the children to this forest-bordered beach? Where are they? Is the land they are on part of a larger land-mass or an island? What is the ruin at the center of the island? What are two soldiers trying to drown in a sack? Who is the dwarf the children rescue? More, who are they to him?; and how can he believe that "mere children" can be the High Kings and Queens of Narnia? Within the dwarf's narrative, the Caspian he tells of is continually being surprised by events: Narnia is far more than it seems; Miraz is quite other than the uncle he knows; his new tutor is a dwarf in disguise; in the woods he escapes to he loses his way and wakes up surrounded by alien creatures. The world keeps changing before him. As for him, the dwarfs and Talking Beasts cannot be quite sure whether to trust a Telmarine and a human of the race that has for so long suppressed them. Then, when he uses the horn of Queen Susan to call the High Kings and Queens back to Narnia, he cannot be certain which of three places they will arrive at. As for the children, their journey toward Caspian is fraught with doubt and uncertainty concerning their direction and whether or not Aslan is there to guide them. All these questionings are answered, which says something about the world of this book in comparison with the lingering mysteries and depths of *The Lion*. So, too, all secrets are laid bare, and everything hidden comes forth, as Miraz's schemes are revealed, the Old Narnians forsake their often literally underground existence and the legend of the High Kings and Queens is made reality.

In this story the questioning comes, as so much else, from the fact that people are cut off from true reality. No one has full knowledge of what is going on: even Miraz is tricked by his henchmen into his downfall. This may be one reason that the children are for so long separated from Caspian and Aslan's How. And under this is the condition whereby "reality" has been limited, or banished. The rulers of Narnia are Telmarines who have shut away the true nature of that world: his tutor, Dr. Cornelius, tells Caspian of the Old Narnia of Talking Beasts and waking trees, dwarfs and giants, fauns and satyrs, gods and centaurs, which was silenced so long ago by the arrival of the invaders (50). Caspian had first heard of this Old Narnia through the tales told to him by his old nurse: and because he would not, like other Telmarines, suppress that knowledge, and told his uncle what he had learned, the nurse was sent away. The Telmarines are levelers of forests and builders of towns, roads, bridges, and schools—not out of a desire to civilize, but out of the more negative urge to suppress wildness, that characteristic of Old Narnia; they are "at war with all wild things" (60). They seek above all to shut out all knowledge of Aslan, the presiding spirit of Narnia; and this, Dr. Cornelius tells Caspian, leads them to reject the sea:

> Your Kings are in deadly fear of the sea because they can never quite forget that in all stories Aslan comes from over the sea. They don't want to go near it and they don't want anyone else to go near it. So they have let great woods grow up to cut their people off from the coast. But because they have quarrelled with the trees they are afraid of the woods. And because they are afraid of the woods they imagine that they are full of ghosts. And the Kings and great men, hating both the sea and the wood, partly believe these stories, and partly encourage them. They feel safer if no one in Narnia dares go down to the coast and look out to sea—towards Aslan's land and the morning and the eastern end of the world. (53)

Divided both from the land, the true Narnia, and from the sea, it is certainly ironic that these people are called *Telmarines* (from Latin *tellus*, "the earth," and *marine*, "of the sea"); odder still when we learn later how they are descendants of seagoing pirates from an island in the South Seas on earth.

There are other severances from reality. Caspian is cut off from the kingship that is rightfully his, and eventually exiled from the court itself. Miraz has divided himself from truth by seizing the kingship and making his son heir to the throne. It is fitting that he himself should lose his life through a piece of duplicity. The Telmarines are removed both from their true world and from any knowledge of it: it is to that "proper" world that they are offered a chance to return by Aslan at the end. And of course the Narnians are deprived of their inheritance, their right to their land, to which they are eventually returned.

The most continuous motif in the story is that of the return of wild nature, however. In rejecting wilderness the Telmarines have tried to bend reality to their image; this is the ultimate form of "appropriation" in the story, and like all the others it is overcome. The process involved is reminiscent of J. R. R. Tolkien's description of the independent power of fantasy itself: "The gems all turn into flowers or flames, and you will be warned that all you had (or knew) was dangerous and potent, not really effectively chained, free and wild; no more yours than they were you."[1] That is the image caught in the freeing of the river-god at Beruna from his chains by the destruction of the bridge built in place of the previous natural ford:

> Bacchus and his people splashed forward into the shallow water, and a minute later the most curious things began happening. Great, strong trunks of ivy came curling up all the piers of the bridge, growing as quickly as a fire grows, wrapping the stones round, splitting, breaking, separating them. The walls of the bridge turned into hedges gay with hawthorn for a moment and then disappeared as the whole thing with a rush and a rumble collapsed into the swirling water. With much splashing, screaming, and laughter the revellers waded or swam or danced across the ford. (170)

We are made aware of wild nature from the very start of *Prince Caspian*. The children are whirled from the "civilization" of a railway station to a jungle-bordered seashore: indeed they are thrust straight into "nature," finding themselves "standing in a woody place—such a woody place that branches were sticking into them and there was hardly room to move" (12). Right from the start, too, the banished woods begin to make their mark. The children struggle out of the woods to a sandy beach and walk along it until eventually, because there is no source of food by the sea, they return to the wood via a stream which they find flowing down to the sea. There again, "They had to stoop under branches and climb over branches, and they blundered through great masses of stuff like rhododendrons and tore their clothes and got their feet wet in the stream" (17). They come to a ruined castle encroached upon by woods, which ivy, grass, and flowers have invaded and, in parts, almost obliterated. Nature, in the shape of a previous promontory now turned island, prevents them from further movement until they save the dwarf Trumpkin and secure the boat. Then again we are aware of landscape as the boat is rowed around the headland and up Glasswater Creek. The gorge that has appeared in the thousand years of Narnian geographical change then causes them continuing difficulty in their attempts to reach Aslan's How.

And Caspian meanwhile? He has gone from the court and "civilization" eventually to reach wooded mountains amid a storm: he feels the hostility of the trees to him, a Telmarine, and as one falls his horse bolts, until Caspian is struck unconscious by an overhanging branch. Thereafter he is very much "with nature": he wakes to find himself underground, surrounded by a badger and two dwarfs. He meets many other Talking Beasts of Old Narnia, again going underground to meet more dwarfs; finally he joins a nighttime dance of Narnian creatures. He chooses to place his army inside a hill, Aslan's How. The children also find themselves in a Narnian forest after they have come ashore up Glasswater Creek. At night Lucy awakes and walks among the trees, feeling that they are old Narnian trees, and that if she could only find the right words (she nearly does) they would awake: "Though there was not a breath of wind they all stirred about her. The rustling noise of the leaves was almost like words" (103). Next day, despite all their attempts to orient themselves, the children become lost in the forest: "They . . . thought they had struck an old path; but if you know anything about woods, you will know that one is always finding imaginary paths" (106). They are attacked by a wild bear and have to kill it; and then carry meat from it with which to nourish themselves. They are pestered by insects and exhausted by the sun. And in this story they are continually hungry.

It is Aslan who liberates the trees, and makes nature still more wild. Aslan is the opposite of all seizing and holding, whether of living things or of ideas. He cannot be cut off from reality because he contains it: he *is* reality. Lucy's spiritual openness enables her to see Aslan: only when they abandon preconceptions about reality—whether of the correct way across the gorge, or of the notion that Lucy may not really have seen Aslan (a similar error was made concerning her sight of Narnia in the previous book)—can the others begin to see the lion. In the presence of Aslan the gorge begins to take on a character beyond that of geography. He proves the only way across it; and it is not till the children trust in him that they can. "He that believeth on the Son hath everlasting life" (John 3:36): Aslan assumes the aspect of a Christ, and the gorge perhaps that breach in nature, certainly that severance from God, that makes mortals slow of trust and blind to the things of the spirit. It recalls the gorge that blocks the progress of the pilgrim John in *The Pilgrim's Regress*, and which only Christ can help *him* to cross: there (but not here) it is "*Peccatum adae*," the original sin of mankind.

Indeed, that gorge is almost a central symbol of the book in its suggestion of spiritual as much as material division. Caspian's flight from the Telmarine court to the wilderness of Old Narnia is, like similar journeys in Shakespeare's pastorals, a suggestion of the gap between "court" and "country," a gap reconciled only when the true court (an Orlando, Imogen, or Perdita) is united to the country and both return to scour out or cure the old. The whole book is full of images of meeting after division—the rare conjunction of the stars Tarva and Alambil (47–49), the High Kings and Queens returning to Narnia, the gradually effected union with Caspian's forces, Caspian's return to the court after exile, the long severance of the Narnians from their inheritance overcome. (Even the constant expletives of Trumpkin the dwarf—"Beards and bedsteads!" "Giants and junipers!" "Wraiths and wreckage!" (39, 96, 133)—portray a union of opposites.) "Society" seems to grow in the book as Caspian, first alone, collects more friends, and as the children and he bring all Narnia back together. Formerly separated individuals come together in the dance of all creatures. What begins with the abrupt whirling of the children into an unknown place in an unknown land ends with them changing back into their school clothes before leaving Narnia; and with Edmund remarking, on his return to the railway station on Earth, "Bother! . . . I've left my new torch in Narnia," as though Narnia was as close as a friend's house—or a home. This motif of division turned to unity and harmony was also seen in *The Lion, the Witch and the Wardrobe*, and we shall find it again at the end of *The Last Battle*.

As division is replaced by meeting, so ignorance turns to sight. Narnia, at first an unknown place whose trees continually obscure vision, becomes progressively clearer; Aslan, only a hint at first to Lucy, is gradually perceived by her and then by the others, until he takes part in the battle and the triumph, at the end presiding over the choice of worlds given to the Telmarines. Caspian has Miraz's true nature revealed to him; perceives his tutor Cornelius to be other than a man; and after some time understands the true nature of what the twisted dwarf Nikabrik stands for. Only Miraz remains blind to the last. In a sense the development of sight remakes Narnia in its true form: what was obscured or hidden is brought to light and restored. The motif is, "For now we see through a glass darkly: but then face to face" (I Cor. 13:12); the childlike state and the implied evolution here is one in reverse, from world-weary adult to imagination-endowed child.

What is restored is a kind of democracy. If in *The Lion, the Witch and the Wardrobe* the Narnians lack humans, here the humans lack the Narnians. The hierarchic sense of *The Lion*, by which man "topped off" the creatures and alone brought the prophecy into being, is here balanced by a more egalitarian view in which kingship is had by free consent of all the people, or not at all, and in which the accent is as much on the "subjects" as on the "ruler." This is a more "political" book, in which we see Caspian gradually gaining acceptance among the Narnians. He is given no coronation in the book, unlike the children in *The Lion:* the concern to the end is still to establish willing subjects, in the choice of worlds given to the Telmarines. As for the High Kings and Queens, they never become other than children or speak in the elevated tones they did in *The Lion:* they have to prove what they are to Trumpkin, and the story accords them no reverence. For in this book it is pride and selfishness that divide, and in particular the desire to control. Here Caspian lets his victory over Miraz be won for him by another: but it is the playing on Miraz's pride by his duplicitous followers that persuades him to venture himself in single combat.

And Miraz's army is to be overcome by a legion of awakened trees. At their triumphal dance at the end, all levels of being in Narnia are brought together, even in the form of various courses of earth on which the trees dine. We end as we began, with the trees and woods: now in the form of a simple wooden doorway through which, first, those of the Telmarines who wish to, and then the children, may return to their places on Earth. The trees, in the way that they come to life, suggest a magic that defies our conceiving; in their long-lost motion they depict the release of life and truth from all forms of appropriation; in their power and menace they convey the danger to man of trying to shut out nature with civilization; in their return they image the pastoral Golden Age restored; and yet, at the same time, in their roots they show that they belong to the world as the Telmarines with their uncertain provenance and their fears of wood, water, and wild, do not.

If the concern of *The Lion* was most centrally with Aslan, that of *Prince Caspian* is with Narnia. In the first book the stage was being set for Narnia to have a history, and there was less attention to the Narnians themselves. But here the country is continuously and immediately present, and the characters are in collision with it. We learn about Narnia in this book, even if it is changed in aspect from the land the children knew before. We have a strong sense of geography, of the interrelation of places; and as said we are continuously being introduced to all the forms of being that make up Narnia. What still seemed a fantastic world for the children at the end of *The Lion* is now much more solidly there, and independent, to the point where it is almost as real as their own world. Later Narnian books are further to explore this now more "substantial" world, now by moving out to its environs. And yet this very "solidification," this conferral of free life on the world of Narnia, is in a way to prepare us for its end in *The Last Battle;* as Narnia itself is uncreated and reveals behind it far deeper and truer Narnias. To quote Tolkien again: "All tales may come true; and yet, at the last, redeemed, they may be as like and as unlike the forms that we give them as Man, finally redeemed, will be like and unlike the fallen that we know."[2]

they come to recognize as Aslan. Aslan sends them back to their own world.

The book is really a series of episodes, a sort of *Odyssey*, with a varying if eventually more specific goal. *The Lion, the Witch and the Wardrobe* was also episodic, but there each piece, or "microplot," made up a larger whole, whereas here what linkage there is is linear, like knots on a string. The first adventure is on the last known Narnian lands, the Lone Islands, where the children are taken to be sold into slavery, and only the ingenuity of Caspian can foil Gumpas, the corrupt governor of the islands, and secure their release. Then, about a month's journey farther east, and after a violent storm, the ship finds haven on a mountainous island. There Eustace discovers a dragon's lair and is himself turned into a dragon when he falls asleep on a hoard of treasure there. He repents his ill nature, but only Aslan can save him so that he can return in his proper form to the ship. Five days' journey farther east, the ship is attacked by a sea serpent, which again ingenuity foils. Each incident till near the end is quite "islanded," with little reference back or forward. Another four days on brings the party to an island where they find a pool of water that turns everything it touches to gold, including one of the Narnian lords they find there, who they deduce must have dived into it. (This is the third of the lords to be traced: the first, Lord Bern, had remained behind on the Lone Islands, and the second, Lord Octesian, had like Edmund been turned into a dragon by sleeping on the treasure hoard.) Caspian is tempted by gold-lust, but restrained and brought to his senses by the others. Further on, they come to another island of strange invisible people ruled by a magician named Coriakin. Lucy climbs to the upper floor of the magician's house in order to remove the spell of invisibility, and there meets Aslan, as well as the wizard. The next adventure of the *Dawn Treader* is at sea, when they rescue from an island in the midst of a great darkness a Narnian lord who implores them to set off at once because this Dark Island is the place where nightmares come true. Aslan intervenes to lead the ship to safety. From this point on we are no longer told the number of days between destinations, and even the constellations in the sky change: the island they come to thereafter is "the beginning of the end of the world." There they find the last three Narnian lords, asleep at a banquet table, where they have lain ever since they quarreled and one took up from the table the same stone knife that the White Witch used to slay Aslan in Narnia. A former star-spirit, Ramandu, tells them that the enchantment can only be broken if someone journeys to the World's End and does not return. And so the ship sails on, to the utter east.

The episodic character of the story is thus also expressed through the geography of a series of islands. But at the same time the central impulse of the story, the pull of the World's End, is imaged in the quest and the journey of the ship. There is a sense of greater "connectedness" as the story proceeds. Aslan intervenes more and more directly. Eustace tells how he removed his dragon's hide from him. He is present in the book of spells Lucy finds in Coriakin's house, helping her fend off the temptation to make herself beautiful. After she has uttered a spell to "make hidden things visible," he appears to her directly. In the form of an albatross he leads the ship away from the mid-sea darkness. In Ramandu we meet someone who knows of Coriakin (also a fallen star) and who has long ago seen what lies ahead, if only "from a great height." All these glimpses and partial visions culminate in the World's End and Aslan's manifestation. And what we reach at the World's End is a continent—no more islands. The sense of the insular has steadily decreased throughout. The islands first encountered (the Lone Islands) can be crossed, but there is less and less inland penetration as the journey progresses (in Ramandu's country, the travelers venture "less than a bowshot from the shore" [162]), until Aslan is met on a beach. Though called an island, that of Coriakin is not felt to be so, being "a low land lying like a cloud" (113), while Ramandu's "country" has "no mountains but many gentle hills" (161). What seems at first uninhabited lands gradually become peopled, first by invisible folk on Coriakin's isle, then by a man obscured by darkness on the Island of Dreams, then by Ramandu and his daughter and the sleeping lords, and later by the mer-people in the sea itself. This process of "peopling" is to be found in many of the Narnia books—most literally in the seeding of newly created Narnia with humans in *The Magician's Nephew*.

Thus there is a sense of increasing expansiveness in the book—

also a recurrent theme in the *Chronicles*. Expansion is present from the start, when what is at first a small picture of a ship gets much larger than the children, before they are overwhelmed by it. This expansiveness is also expressed in the very journey of the ship, which is voyaging eastward into the utter unknown. As a moral ideal this adventurousness, this confrontation with the threat, menace, and exhilaration of wild experience, is best put by Reepicheep: "This is a very great adventure, and no danger seems to me so great as that of knowing when I get back to Narnia that I left a mystery behind me through fear" (166). But the morality goes beyond this. To be islanded is ultimately to be shut in on the self. Gumpas, the governor of the Lone Islands, is a bureaucrat cut off from the world outside, refusing to acknowledge or even remember the suzerainty of Narnia, indifferent to the moral and human implications of the slave trade going on with his sanction, unavailable to the people, and then only by appointment or "between nine and ten PM on second Saturdays" every month (52–53). As for the sailors of the Lone Islands, they know little or nothing of what lies to the east. Eustace's selfishness is depicted symbolically at the next island reached, in what amounts to a spiritual landscape: he loses himself in a fog in a deep and inaccessible cleft in the mountains and then sleeps in a dragon's cave on the pile of loot he finds; thereafter, he is locked in dragon-form, unable to communicate more than sketchily with the others. Even this sketchiness however is better than his previous refusal to speak with them: now he is at least trying. The next island again has a symbol of possession in the form of the gold-making pool that almost makes Caspian forget himself. On Coriakin's island, the unseen people, or Dufflepuds, are invisible to one another through their own stupidity: Coriakin himself has been confined there with them as punishment. The lord shut in darkness on the island of dreams is enclosed in his own subconscious and its terrors. The three lords asleep at the table in Ramandu's island are victims of their own contentiousness.

Set against this is Aslan, who unpeels Eustace from his dragon-coat, helps guard Lucy against the temptations to selfishness of Coriakin's book of spells, leads the *Dawn Treader* out of the mid-sea darkness, and appears to Caspian to bid him look to his duties and abandon his sudden resolution to forsake all and go to the World's End. And another countersymbol is the ship itself, with its cooperative society of people manning and defending it. While Eustace is unreformed, he keeps to his cabin or his bed for much of the time; by contrast Reepicheep is constantly on deck, near the lookout on the prow. It is the *Dawn Treader* that by its voyage links together all the separate islands. The ship also brings them into being, as it were, by discovering them for Narnia; for the object is to return after the voyage. This is figured in the map created by Coriakin:

> He laid two blank sheets of parchment on the table and asked Drinian [the captain] to give him an exact account of their voyage up to date: and as Drinian spoke, everything he described came out on the parchment in fine clean lines till at last each sheet was a splendid map of the Eastern Ocean, showing Galma, Terebinthia, the Seven Isles, the Lone Islands, Dragon Island, Burnt Island, Deathwater, and the land of the Duffers itself, all exactly the right sizes and in the right positions. (148)

*The Voyage of the "Dawn Treader"* is itself a map, a series of narrative connections in prose. The very thematic connections and patterns in the book are a "social" counterpoise to selfishness and isolation.

Another main theme in *The Voyage of the "Dawn Treader"* is the relationship between fiction and the real world. What takes the children to Narnia is a fiction come to life, a picture of a ship. Eustace has been brought up to eschew fiction. "He liked books if they were books of information and had pictures of grain elevators or of fat foreign children doing exercises in model schools" (9; that "foreign" is an unfortunate lapse on Lewis's part). Aboard the *Dawn Treader*, he cannot believe in the reality of the ship, or else disparages it in favor of steamships or submarines; he demands to see the local British Consul; he is ironically exposed through his diary, where he rebukes the others for "pretending" that the (perfectly normal) waves are not a storm, "Huge waves keep coming in over the front and I have seen the boat nearly go under any number of times. All the others pretend to take no notice of this, either from swank or because as Harold [his father] says one of the most cowardly things ordinary people do is to shut their eyes to Facts" (31). He thinks there is only one reality, the modern world on earth, and thus he ignores "Facts" in trying to ignore or deny the reality of Narnia. On the way to Dragon Island, Eustace is still to be found complaining that the ship is without a radio or a thermometer (64, 65). Not surprisingly his diary is soon a series of self-deluding lies. It is quite ironic to hear him lecturing Caspian and the others against the dangers of "wishful thinking" in their search for new lands east of the Lone Islands (66). When Eustace gets up to steal some of the dwindling water supply and tiptoes out of the cabin to avoid waking Caspian and Edmund, he tells us that this was in kindness to them for their recent lack of sleep: "I always try to consider others whether they are nice to me or not" (66). Eustace's redemption is brought about by his being turned into a creature of fiction, a dragon. He is forced to live for a time in a giant scaly body, to run on all fours, and to struggle to write in the sand with huge claws. He is also given the pleasure of flight, but that is nothing to his alienation from the others: the company he previously refused to acknowledge he is now all too desperate to obtain. By living a fantasy he has come to realize true "fact," that more realities than one are possible. In its degree, this idea of living through a fantasy to realize true fact is the experience of all the children who enter Narnia.

Severance from fact is also evident in the Dufflepuds, whose very invisibility from one another suggests it. These people are simply stupid. They grew to dislike their admittedly grotesque appearance when visible; but now, having been unseen for so long, they wish to regain visibility. The magician who turned them into monopods[1] did so because they would refuse to gather water from the stream rather than from its farther source the spring, so that they went to unnecessary trouble and continually muddied the water. This stupidity is reminiscent of the projectors in Swift's *Gulliver's Travels:* the Magician says, "You wouldn't believe the troubles I've had with them. A few months ago they were all for washing up the plates and knives before dinner: they said it saved time afterwards. I've caught them planting boiled potatoes to save cooking them when they were dug up. One day the cat got into the dairy and twenty of them were at work moving all the milk out; no one thought of moving the cat" (141). They all continually agree with every word of their verbose "Chief," and can even agree to diametric opposites one after the other. They are an extraordinary mixture of the fantastic and the banal, small dwarfs each with a single gigantic foot, and yet without the smallest degree of imagination. It is Reepicheep who reconciles them to their grotesque shapes by showing them how they can use their feet as canoes on the sea.

Indeed a major theme of *The Voyage of the "Dawn Treader"* is the use of the imagination, and how it can extend rather than ignore reality. This book is actually the most "practical" of the *Chronicles of Narnia*: we are continually being made aware of how things work on the ship, an artifice of man which forms a center of attention. Then again there is the practicality of Caspian as leader. He invents a fictional fleet with which to deceive Gumpas, and he uses crafty rhetoric to reverse the refusal of many of his men to follow him to the World's End. Even Reepicheep, for all his impetuousness in the most impossible situations, is the one who finds that the best way for the *Dawn Treader* to escape from the closing coils of the great sea serpent is by slipping the ship through them, and who finds a use for the Dufflepuds' feet. This we can call the practical imagination. Another and different form of it is the book of spells of Coriakin, by which wizardy can be used to adjust reality, whether to become invisible, to be the most beautiful being in existence, to overlook other's opinions of oneself, or simply to cure warts. More terrible is the self-devouring imagination of the island where dreams come true: here nothing is accomplished save the undying terror of the passive subject.

There are several layers of imagination in the book. First there is the book itself as a product of C. S. Lewis's imagination: he has made the fiction that contains the worlds of England and of Narnia. He frequently enters his narrative—more so arguably than in any other of the *Chronicles*, thus reminding us of the other "reality" from which he is writing: "By the way, I have never yet heard how these remote islands became attached to the crown of Narnia; if I ever do, and if the story is at all interesting, I may put it in some other book" (36); "What awaited them on this island was going to concern Eustace more than anyone else, but it cannot be told in his words because after

September 11 he forgot about keeping his diary for a long time" (68). Then there is the imagined world of Narnia and of the adventure of the *Dawn Treader*, which turns out within the book to be as "real" as our own world: this is Eustace's journey of understanding. Then each adventure of the ship on its way to the World's End is a separate imagined world on its own. The book is peculiar for creating one strange adventure after another, from the story of Eustace's transformation, Coriakin's country with the extraordinary Dufflepuds, or Ramandu's land with its strange sleepers and birds, to the amazingly clear, sweet water on the way to World's End, the mer-people with their inverted lives beneath the waves, the sea of white water lilies, the great standing wave and the huge mountains that rise behind the sun. Each of these by its very invented nature puts a particular premium on the imagination.

Then we have changing levels of "fantasy." First we shift from this world to the Narnian ship. Then, to the Narnians, the journey on which they are embarked is taking them to places that are unknown and mysterious, and to being they would regard as at least part fantastic in relation to *their* reality—sea serpents, wizards, dragons, a retired star, mer-people. More than this, the kinds of fantastic episode themselves change. The Lone Islands are less mysterious than they at first appear: they are inhabited by corrupt man, and they are "Lone" not just because of geographical isolation, but because through greed and torpor their inhabitants have cut themselves off from Narnia and from knowledge of any land to the east of them. Dragon Island presents us with fantasy operating at a primarily moral level, even if Aslan is reportedly present. The old and dying dragon Eustace sees is really the enchanted Lord Octesian: as Eustace will be, he was supposedly turned into a dragon through the greed symbolized in its hoard. Eustace, more fortunate, is morally educated and ultimately restored to human shape. The sea serpent is a piece of *Arabian Nights* fantasy: apparently terrible, it is made ludicrously stupid in its abortive attempt to crush the ship in its coils. The threat of evil and death in the gold-making water of the pool on the next island strikes a much deeper note: here is magic that seems joined to darker forces in the world. With Coriakin and the Dufflepuds, we are, in one way, back with a lighter side of fantasy:

but at the same time Aslan's presence, and his clear responsibility for Coriakin's being on the island and having to put up with the Dufflepuds, suggests some more mysterious reality. Lucy's temptation with the book of spells again keeps the fantasy at a moral level, but we are much closer here than we were with Eustace to the temptation itself and the movements of the spirit; further Aslan's action and presence are more immediate. (Incidentally, the temptations of Lucy here are more "sophisticated" than with Edmund in *The Lion, the Witch and the Wardrobe*: there it was simple greed, but here it is the more social and even adolescent temptation to be beautiful or to know what others think of one.[2]) With Coriakin, too, we have reached a wizard who can alter reality with his spells: here the very nature of the fantasy-making capacity seems to be questioned, and indicted wherever it operates out of egoism or selfishness.

In Ramandu's country what was wonder in the creating imagination has changed to something nearer to miracle. Ramandu is a "retired" star who is visited every morning by a flock of strange birds, one of which gives him a fire berry that helps to make him grow younger[3]—the ideal of development in the *Chronicles*. The three lords who lie asleep at his table have through lifting the evil stone knife there tasted the mystery of iniquity. What the whole episode means is no longer quite clear: positioned where it is, at "The Beginning of the End of the World," it marks the point where magic turns to mysticism. The sense of the mysterious grows as we journey through the clear ocean and the sea of water lilies to the great standing wave. And at the end, at the farthest point where the sky meets the earth, what has been "invention" becomes scriptural reality: the fantasy that has been this story and all that it has in it merges into that larger Christian fantasy of the Gospels, which is Truth itself. On the other side of the standing wave, on a grassy shore, the children find a lamb standing by a fire on which fish are roasting. The lamb is the Lamb of God, the same God who divided the Red Sea for the Israelites, and who beside an identical meal appeared as the risen Christ to His disciples in John 21: 9–13 to ask, as here, " 'Come and have breakfast' "; and this lamb who is also a lion draws on those images of lion and lamb (even Old Testament God and risen Christ) that are part of the Bible and long hallowed in Christian tradition. From this perspective we begin to see the journey of the ship to the east in rather new terms—as an approach to that Christ who is eternal sunrise and resurrection. Thus the total voyage has been deeper and further into the more remote imagination, and yet that imagination culminates in supreme reality: correspondingly, all along the way that what we might think fiction can be fact. The idea of going "farther up and farther in" through different levels of fantasy or magic to divine fact is a recurrent one in the *Chronicles*.

The book suggests another connection between the imagination and reality, or rather, image and truth. The voyage, the story's progression, is one full of anticipation, where our minds continually reach forward to wonder at the next possibility. Each island has for the time a blaze of mystery, both as it is part of the unknown, and as we wonder whether it will be close to the World's End. Each appearance of Aslan—possibly in a dream to Eustace, through a book of spells to Lucy, in the form of an albatross at the Island of Dreams, or to Caspian alone in his cabin—anticipates that fuller knowledge of him that awaits at World's End. The wonder, the fantasy alone, of the strange places visited loosens the fixed habits of our minds, opens them to that larger experience. And then there is the experience of Romantic *Sehnsucht*: the feeling that certain images in our experience can act as relays for a numinous reality both in and beyond them, an experience always associated with desire and longing, in Lewis' work ultimately for heaven. The way this story slips from wondrous image to image in the act of voyaging itself enacts what Lewis saw as the course of desire itself, quickened by one image but lost if that image is clung to.[4] The image is most poignant as the rowboat with the children and Reepicheep in it crosses the last of the sea of lilies and approaches the giant rainbow-colored wave between them and the World's End:

> Suddenly there came a breeze from the east, tossing the top of the wave into foamy shapes and ruffling the smooth water all round them. It lasted only a second or so but what it brought them in that second none of those three children will ever forget. It brought both

a smell and a sound, a musical sound. Edmund and Eustace would never talk about it afterwards. Lucy could only say, "It would break your heart." "Why," said I, "was it so sad?" "Sad! No," said Lucy.

No one in that boat doubted that they were seeing beyond the End of the World into Aslan's country. (206)

After that the imagery is scriptural: emotion exists only in distance, but the thing itself is wondrous beyond wonder.[5] At the same time too the imagination goes from the miraculous and the mysterious to the paradoxical that defeats imagination: a wave thirty feet high that stands forever, a grassy sward where the sky meets the earth, a range of mountains beyond the sun.

# 8

# The Silver Chair

*The Silver Chair* is the most "controlled" of the Narnia books. Curiously, it begins in a context of total lack of control, a boarding school called Experiment House, which follows the "enlightened" approach of letting children do just what they like:[1] the result is that the older pupils take to bullying the younger ones, with little hindrance from the school authorities, apart from the occasional "friendly chat" with the headmaster, who treats offenders sympathetically, as having psychological rather than disciplinary problems. The book starts with one of the victims of this bullying, a girl named Jill Pole, crying behind the gym. She is joined by Eustace Scrubb, whom we met in *The Voyage of the "Dawn Treader,"* and he gradually succeeds in comforting her. Eventually, and shyly, he tells her about his experiences in Narnia, and when she has managed to suspend her disbelief, they both resolve to escape from the horrors of the school into that fantastical realm. thus they go from being more or less at the mercy of a system to taking control of their own destinies.

They stand side by side in the shrubbery, facing east, holding their hands out palms down in front of them (as did Ramandu and his daughter in *The Voyage of the "Dawn Treader,"* 173), and first Eustace, then Jill, chants, "Aslan, Aslan, Aslan!" What they then hear is the crowd of school bullies in pursuit of them. They flee through the shrubbery toward a high wall that surrounds the school grounds, a wall with a door in it that leads to a wide heath beyond, but a door that is only rarely open. Once there they find the door closed, but on turning the handle Eustace finds that it opens. And beyond it is not the heath but a beautiful bright, warm land of great trees and glades and wondrously colored singing birds. They enter this realm, and all the sounds and sights of their former world entirely disappear. This country will turn out to be Aslan's land, and he is to tell Jill, "You would not have called to me unless I had been calling to you" (28). Despite Aslan's statement, this scene contrasts markedly with the mode of entry into Narnia in the other books—in *The Lion* there is the "chance" concealment in the wardrobe during a game of hide-and-seek; in *Prince Caspian* the children are summoned to Narnia when Caspian blows Queen Susan's horn; in *The Voyage* the children fall into a picture of a sailing ship that suddenly becomes real; in *The Magician's Nephew* the child-protagonists are tricked by their magician-uncle into using some magic rings he has made to travel to other worlds, and these worlds are selected largely by "chance"; in *The Last Battle* the children are drawn back to Narnia partly through the pleas of the hard-pressed King Tirian, but more immediately through their deaths in a railway accident. But in *The Silver Chair* the children are seen as willing their passage to the other realm.

And here too the narrative is itself far more markedly outlined and delimited from the outset. A specific quest is set before the children by Aslan: they are to find and rescue the long-lost prince and heir apparent of Narnia, Rilian, stolen from his father, King Caspian, many years back; and they are to pursue this end until either they have achieved it or died in the attempt, or returned to their own world (28–29). In all the other Narnia stories the part they are to play is gradually discovered by the children: here it is laid bare from the start, and is indeed one "laid on" them. The children are told that this quest may be readily brought to a conclusion if they heed four particular signs: first, Eustace must speak to an old friend he will meet on first setting foot in Narnia; second, the children must travel north to the ruined city of the ancient giants; third, when they arrive there they will find written instructions on a stone and they must follow those instructions; and fourth, they must recognize the person who calls for help in Aslan's name as the true prince. It will turn out that the children do not obey these injunctions readily, but the series of their duties gives a preordained structure to their journey.

Self-control is one of the book's major themes. When Jill and Eustace first arrive in Aslan's land, they walk through the woods until they find themselves on the verge of an immense precipice. Eustace, afraid of heights, backs away, but Jill, who has no such fear, goes still nearer the edge. Gazing at the treacherous drop, she too tries to step back; but finds she cannot, for her legs have gone like putty and everything is swimming before her eyes. Sensing her in danger of falling off, Eustace rushes forward to grab her, but "by now she had no control over her own arms and legs" (22), and in the confusion it is Eustace who plunges into the gulf. (He is then saved by Aslan.) Jill's lack of self-control has consequences that extend beyond herself, endangering both her and her companion. In "recompense" for this lapse, her meeting with Aslan is to be accomplished through self-subjugation: she is extremely thirsty and wishes to drink from a brook, but to do so she must approach the lion; once again her body is frozen with fear (25). She must overcome her terror and trust the lion before she can touch a drop of water.

Throughout the story efforts of will are important, particularly for Jill, who is not used to Narnia. Eustace, feeling its air, is capable of a courage and hardiness beyond a child's means. It is actually from Jill's point of view that much of the story is written. She later finds it difficult to be taken from the comfortable room in a Narnian palace where she is sleeping to a midnight conference with owls, followed by a flight on an owl's back to marshlands, all the time having to pinch herself to stay awake and not fall off. The children's guide beyond Narnia, a bizarre creature called a Marsh-wiggle, has a habitually gloomy view of things, which serves to bolster their courage and willpower: where he looks everywhere for disasters, they reply with compensatory cheer that sees them through many difficulties. Self-control is needed as the group passes by the giants of the northern waste of Ettinsmoor, who waken and begin hurling great boulders—not at them, as the children think, but rather at a cairn that the giants are using as a cockshy. Puddleglum (the Marsh-wiggle) tells them not to look at the giants nor to run, lest they be seen and pursued at once, "So they kept on, pretending not to have seen the giants. It was like walking past the gate of a house where there is a fierce dog, only far worse" (74). The giants themselves are images of lack of self-control, as they soon lose their tempers and start hitting one another and then begin crying like babies when they are hurt.

The band next encounters a beautiful lady in the company of a knight in black armor. When they tell her they are looking for the "City Ruinous" of the giants, she tells them she cannot help them, but instead directs them to the castle of Harfang, home of "the gentle giants" (80). There, excellent hospitality and warmth are promised to the children. Despite Puddleglum's warnings, Harfang soon becomes the objective of all of them, and it is partly because of this that they fail to recognize the ancient giant city as they pass it in a snowstorm on their way to Harfang. But Harfang, which seems so free, open, and welcoming, is actually a trap, for unknown to the group the lady has sent them not as guests of the giants' impending Autumn Feast but as one of its main courses. Here again there is inversion: their own greed has made them subject to the greed of others. And only when this has happened do they realize that they overlooked the signs of the City Ruinous and the written instructions, "UNDER ME," which with more care and trust in Aslan they might have discovered before their entrapment. Again, they must exercise self-control to escape from Harfang. They must appear to be happy and ignorant of their captors' designs, to put the giants off guard, and, as with their encounter with the giants of Ettinsmoor, when they finally succeed in getting out of the castle, they must not run (117). Later, in the realm of Underland, Jill, who suffers from claustrophobia and fear of darkness, has to put up with her fill of them in the endless caverns.

Self-control and willpower are again at issue when the group meet the enchanted Prince Rilian. At first he appears as a rather priggish devotee of the Queen of Underland and is not recognizable as Rilian at all. He tells them that for an hour every day he has a fit, and in his madness utters all sorts of falsehoods about himself—during this time he must be fettered in a silver chair. He warns them to pay no heed to his demands in this state, and that should they release him, he will do them harm. The "fit" duly comes upon him, during which he proclaims himself a wretched slave doomed to years in this dark Underland and cries to be released. The others force themselves to resist his blandishments. Finally he adjures them to set him free, "By all fears and all loves, by the bright skies of Overland, by the great Lion, by Aslan himself . . ." (144). These are at least the words of the fourth sign the children were to look for, and they are put in a quandary. Eventually they and the Marsh-wiggle resolve that they must now obey the wishes of the captive, even if it means their own deaths, and thus they release him. Their obedience here allows the young man to realize himself as Rilian and his home as Narnia, indeed to come to himself.

The theme of control is of course central to Rilian's experience with the witch. He lost his mother to an evil serpent on which he vowed revenge, but the serpent later appeared to him as a beautiful lady, capturing first his heart and then his body, which is lodged a virtual prisoner in Underland. We learn that Rilian's mother died before she could tell him something; we may guess that that "something" was not to lose control over himself and become obsessed with seeking vengeance; for it is precisely loss of power over himself that puts him in the power of others—a motif we have seen elsewhere in the story. Loss of power characterizes Underland. The Earthmen there work silently, without animation, in virtual darkness, the vegetation is sickly, and whole caverns are full of motionless, sleeping creatures. Rilian is to be the witch's tool for seizing power in Overland, which is actually, and unknown to him, his own country of Narnia, the realm he in any case has the lineal authority to govern. The control the witch exerts is tyranny: she destroys selves and allows no free will. This contrasts with Aslan, who authorizes a quest that can only be realized by people acting independently out of free choice, willingly to subjugate their selfhood and trust in him. Self-control here is a good; control of the self from outside evil. Bound to the silver chair when most truly himself, and free only when under the control of the queen, Rilian is an emblem of self-control gone wrong; all that can save him is grace, embodied in Aslan's "gift" to him of the children and Puddleglum.

But Rilian's freedom from the chair, and his self-realization, are not the end of the story. As the group are about to make their escape, the witch confronts them and proceeds by means of enchantment to overwhelm their wills. A soporific powder she throws on the fire makes them unable to think clearly. She begins to convince them, while playing hypnotically monotonous chords on a mandolin, that there is no Narnia, no Overland, no sun, no world outside Narnia, for all is dream, mere solipsism. Gradually they all come to believe her—even, despite long resistance, Puddleglum. Finally she tells them that there is no Aslan. At this last act, Puddleglum summons his remaining strength, walks over to the fire and, with disregard for his own flesh, thrusts his foot into it in an attempt to "extinguish" the queen's power. At this the enchantment begins to break and the witch's control over them to crack. She ceases to hypnotize them with words and insults the Marsh-wiggle directly. His head cleared, he now begins to answer her. And his victorious answer finally throws her back within her true self, and she changes to serpent shape and attempts to crush Rilian in her coils, (rather like Error in Spenser's *The Faerie Queene*). Assisted by the others, Rilian kills the snake. Thus, self-control defeats tyranny.

Just as the tyranny of the witch is overthrown, so, at the end of the story, is that of the bullies of the school, Experiment House, from which the children initially fled. They return, as is the Narnia way, at exactly the moment they left, but now empowered. Aslan breaks down part of the wall round the school, and sits with his back to our world, a symbol of strength. And through this gap, accompanied by Caspian, who through Aslan's grace has been victorious even over death, walk the children, to administer such chastisement and put such fear into the bullies before them that never again will they or anyone else be victimized in that school. The headmaster is replaced, ten of the bullies expelled, and "from that day forth things changed for the better at Experiment House, and it became quite a good school" (206).

This is the only one of the Narnia books to continue the action that occurs within the "other" world into our own. In *The Magician's Nephew* the boy-protagonist Digory is able to revive his sick mother on earth with a Narnian apple, and there are numerous incursions between our and other worlds including Narnia, but there the point is the commerce, the intercommunication between worlds. In *The*

*Silver Chair* the link is more causal. Further, the action at Experiment House that begins the book is completed at the end. This is suggestive of another theme central to *The Silver Chair*, the distinction between reality and illusion, where the children must keep a grasp on reality and fend off illusion. The most obvious forms of this are the way the children have to remember and recognize the four signs, and the theme of enchantment as it relates to Rilian. Thus, because Caspian does not appear as the boy he knew but as an old king, Eustace does not recognize him and the first sign is missed: only later, when the witch is overthrown and the children are transported back to Aslan's land, is Caspian returned through a drop of Aslan's blood to the boy that Eustace knew. As we have seen, the children do follow the second sign and travel north to the ruined city of the giants, but they do not recognize it when they are there, and only know it for what it is when they are trapped in Harfang. They are able to obey the third sign partly because they are chased into hiding under the city by the hounds of the giants. And with Puddleglum's help they are able to recognize the true Rilian and withstand the witch's attempts to persuade them that their "reality" is an illusion. Their journey downward to Underland is in both a literal and metaphoric sense a journey to bedrock. Illusions multiply around them, but it is in the depths of the earth that they are able finally and fully to obey Aslan's crucial injunction, to release the young man who calls for help in his name. Indeed there is a gradation in performance with regard to the signs: the children fail to perceive the first sign; the second sign is overlooked and only recognized when it is nearly too late; the third is followed part by choice and part by accident; but the fourth is recognized and courageously acted upon.

The book is thus full of deceptions and illusions that must be penetrated, from Caspian to Harfang to Rilian. The serpent appears as a beautiful woman to Rilian and entraps him in a web of enchantment. The giants of Ettinsmoor at first look like huge boulders. The lady the children meet out riding beyond Ettinsmoor "charms" them and directs them to Harfang. In the snowstorm (perhaps symbolic of their own moral confusion) in which the group crosses the ruined city of the giants, they find and follow some strange trenches in the flat, stone area, which come to dead ends: these are actually part of the sign "UNDER ME," but they miss the significance of this. The Earthmen of Underland seem gloomy and cold, and the whole notion of being under the earth suggests entrapment and misery: yet, with the overthrow of the witch's enchantments, the Earthmen prove to have been tyrannized automata, originally from a deeper and fiery level of Underland called Bism: they now come to excited and noisy life and descend from the dark and silent lands to which they have been confined, into a land of white-hot salamanders and living gems (175–76).[2]

*The Silver Chair* is a highly elemental book, further emphasizing the importance of the "real." Just as there are four signs that will guide toward the truth, so we are made aware of the four elements that make up physical reality. On their journey from Aslan's high country to Narnia, the children travel through wide air, on the breath of Aslan. Arrived in Narnia, they find themselves beside water, as the old king sets sail; and they are to return to it at the end, when he comes back in his ship. The Marsh-wiggle lives in a landscape broken up by water channels. The overthrow of the witch produces a flood in Underland. For earth we need look no further than the realm of Underland, the gloomy Earthmen, and, last, the struggle out of a high earth bank back into Narnia. And there are several images of fire, whether at the Marsh-wiggle's wigwam, or in Harfang, and most particularly the enchanted fire of the witch and the fiery realm of Bism. The children are often described in this book as being affected by the various climates.

One difference between this book and *The Voyage of the "Dawn Treader"* is that here we travel not toward Aslan's land but away and down from it. And the journey is not eastward to the sunrise and clarity, but west, into sunset and darkness. Indeed, much of the journeying in this book is done in darkness or obscurity. The medium is increasingly the obfuscating one of this world, where it is hard to tell truth from falsehood or to determine one's true spiritual way. Aslan warned Jill of the thickening lower air that could confuse her mind (30). If in *The Voyage* the landscape becomes increasingly more clear and stark, with the sun so bright and the sea so clear that one can see right down to the shadow of the *Dawn Treader* running along the bottom, in *The Silver Chair* the children can barely see in front of them in the near-darkness of Underland, and Rilian begs to be returned to the upper world where "There used to be a little pool. When you looked down into it you could see all the trees growing upside-down in the water, all green, and below them, deep, very deep, the blue sky" (142). In Underland the travelers come to a place where the sharpness and determinacy of objects and language alike seem finally all but lost, to a great cavern "full of a dim drowsy radiance" with "some kind of moss" on the floor, in which are growing flabby plants that seem part tree, part mushroom; and among these are lying a number of indeterminate animals either asleep or dead (125–26). There is a series of negations as they cross this place: "The bare feet of the gnomes, padding on the deep moss, made no sound. There was no wind, there were no birds, there was no sound of water. There was no sound of breathing from the strange beasts" (126). There is striking contrast to this landscape in the portrayal of the bright trees, glades and many-colored singing birds of Aslan's land, when the children first enter it (19–20).

One of the most memorable characters in the book is the Marsh-wiggle Puddleglum, who guides the children on their way. Modeled as he may be on the gardener, Fred Paxford, at the Kilns, Lewis's Oxford dwelling, he is certainly very much in contact with the ground, on which he has his webbed feet firmly placed. He is far quicker than the children to see through deceivers. He is an outdoor, Crusoe-like creature, very much a solitary figure, living like other Marsh-wiggles in an isolated wigwam in the midst of a wetland full of birds and surrounded by "landscape"—hills to north and east, a forest to south and west. He is so much a part of his environment that the children cannot see him when he is fishing, for he sits so still and is "nearly the same colour as the marsh" (63). He is preeminently a creature of the open air and an ideal guide, for he knows the land very well. He is thus particularly in touch with reality and thus least likely to be susceptible to illusion. Indeed, his forte is not illusion but disillusion: he has a propensity for looking on the bad side of things. He tells the children when they first meet him.

> Why, it's not in reason that you should like our sort of victuals, though I've no doubt you'll put a bold face on it. All the same, while

I am a catching of them, if you two could try to light the fire—no harm trying—! The wood's behind the wigwam. It may be wet. You could light it inside the wigwam, and then we'd get all the smoke in our eyes. Or you could light it outside, and then the rain would come and put it out. Here's my tinder-box. You won't know how to use it, I expect. (65)

One of the finest touches is the Marsh-wiggle's pipe, which has such heavy black tobacco (perhaps mixed with mud) that the smoke does not rise in the air but "trickled out of the bowl and downwards and drifted along the ground like a mist" (66): it might fairly be called glum tobacco. Puddleglum meets his match in the gloominess of the Earthmen of Underland, however. As he remarks, "If these chaps don't teach me to take a serious view of life, I don't know what will" (124). In Underland he is much more cheering to the children. It is not really that he is gloomy at all: it is that in allowing for the worst, he is inclusive of possibility, and his presentiments are sometimes realized.[3] It is precisely this that is behind his extraordinary riposte to the witch-queen's assertion that everything concerning Narnia, sunlight and open air, is a dream. He tells her that if it is one, then it is one that beats her dreary Underland world hollow; her world may be the real one, but if the others have simply "made up" Narnia and the sun, then their illusory world is far better then her "real" one. "That's why I'm going to stand by the play-world. I'm on Aslan's side even if there isn't any Aslan to lead it. I'm going to live as like a Narnian as I can even if there isn't any Narnia" (156–57). The Marsh-wiggle is only superficially gloomy, just as the glamour of the witch is only an appearance. Her reductiveness is of quite another order from his mournful pragmatism.

When the Marsh-wiggle embraces the real, while paradoxically advocating illusion, illusion is shattered. The witch becomes the serpent she is, the children and Rilian come to themselves, and with the breaking of the spells of the witch the Earthmen realize their true natures and home once more. It seems somehow appropriate that a book so founded on the ideas of "illusion" and "reality" should be so literary in its orientation, especially to Milton's *Comus* and to

Spenser's *The Faerie Queene* (Book 2, in Mammon's cave) for the episode on Rilian bound to the silver chair, or to the fraudulent Duessa of *The Faerie Queene* book 1, S. T. Coleridge's *Christabel*, or John Keats's *Lamia* for the idea of the serpentine enchantress of the woods.[4] As well as springing out of other stories, this story feeds back into still larger narrative patterns. In the journey of the children into Underworld from Aslan's country and back again, we have something of what the critic Northrop Frye has, in his *The Secular Scripture: A Study of the Structure of Romance*, called the four main narrative movements in literature: "first, the descent from a higher world; second, the descent to a lower world; third, the ascent from a lower world; and, fourth, the ascent to a higher world." And, in more detail, Frye describes the descent as "a growing confusion of identity and of restrictions on action. There is a break in consciousness at the beginning, with analogies to falling asleep, followed by a descent to a lower world which is sometimes a world of cruelty and imprisonment. . . . In the descent there is a growing isolation and immobility: charms and spells hold one motionless; human beings are turned into subhuman creatures, and made more mechanical in behaviour; hero or heroine are trapped in labyrinths or prisons." As for ascent, this involves "escape, remembrance, or discovery of one's real identity, growing freedom, and the breaking of enchantment."[5] The whole cycle can be seen as part of the myth of the initiation of the hero.

But the ultimate story in which it is subsumed as has been well-pointed out,[6] is that which is found in the Gospels, the story in which, as the Apostles' Creed has it, Christ was "born of the Virgin Mary; suffered under Pontius Pilate, was crucified, dead, and buried; he descended into hell; the third day he rose again from the dead; he ascended into heaven, and sitteth on the right hand of God the Father Almighty." That story subsumes all other patterns, whether the cycle of the seasons, or the Fall of Man from Grace and His Redemption. The story moves from the summer of Aslan's country down to the autumn of Narnia, thence to winter during the journey, and finally back to "midsummer sunshine" on the Mountain of Aslan. So too it can be seen in its way as partaking in the story of the Fall of Man in the yielding of the children to the blandishments of the witch, and redemption through Aslan's name; but more still in the portrait of Rilian, whose sensuality led him into bondage to the evil of the witch, a paralysis of the will from which he could only be liberated by the gracious gift of Aslan in the shape of the children and Puddleglum. There is also a pattern of increasing enclosure, from Harfang to Underland to the prison rooms and the chair; this followed in a sudden release, as Bism is opened up and the children break out into Narnia and farther out still to Aslan's country again.

Just as the story goes deeper down into the realm of enchantment and deception, so it is permeated by reality, and so too its pattern partakes in a larger reality. The idiom is one of paradox: the way down is the way up, the journey through illusion is the only way to truth. And Aslan can be most present in his seeming absence: it is of course no accident that the original verses inscribed by the former vainglorious ruler of the ruined city of the giants as his epitaph— "Though under Earth and throneless now I be, / Yet, while I lived, all Earth was under me" (134)—have been obliterated apart from the last two words, which make up the third sign the children were given by Aslan to look out for.

In this book, in contrast to *The Voyage of the "Dawn Treader,"* the imagination is seen as dangerous and something to be distrusted. In *The Voyage*, the whole progress of the book was in a sense deeper and deeper into the imagination. One of its central themes was the value of "fiction" over "fact." In *The Silver Chair* it is reality that must be kept clearly in view. And yet there is no final contradiction. The journey of *The Silver Chair* is into the world; and in *The Voyage of the "Dawn Treader"* it is out of it. Magicians in *The Voyage* are on spiritual probation. Enchantment is a good because it is founded in the holy truth that is Aslan. But in *The Silver Chair* enchantment is evil not just because we journey into the murky air of the world, but because it emanates from the witch, from falsehood. Thus, imagination is not to be valued in and of itself, and a slavish adherence to reality or "fact," in Eustace's materialistic notion of it in *The Silver Chair*, is equally to be avoided. But in both books the concern with what is real, and with getting close to it, is central. And this is a recurrent theme throughout the *Chronicles of Narnia*. In *The Magician's Nephew* Narnia is given its self in being created; in *The Lion, the Witch and the Wardrobe* and *Prince Caspian* it is restored to its true nature from a perverted state; in *The Last Battle* it is given a still truer series of realities beyond its death; in *The Voyage of the "Dawn Treader"* we journey toward the reality that underlies all our fictions; and in *Prince Caspian*, *The Silver Chair*, and *The Horse and His Boy*, variously dispossessed princes are given back or rediscover their true identities. For Lewis, the theme is so vital precisely because of the premium he placed on the imagination as a route to divine reality: once give way to the enchantment of the image rather than its source and one is lost, a slave ultimately to the father of lies. The common feature of the damned in Lewis's *The Great Divorce* (1945) is their self-delusion, nowhere more strikingly seen than in their incapacity to perceive the overpowering reality of heaven when it is right before them.

# 9

## The Horse and His Boy

This story takes us back in time to the reign of the High Kings and Queens of Narnia after the defeat of the White Witch, described in *The Lion, the Witch and the Wardrobe*. Like the next book, *The Magician's Nephew*, which tells of the creation of Narnia, this book interrupts the sequence of the *Chronicles*, and with it the purposiveness attached to linear progression. Life, Lewis seems to be saying, is more random than we often care to admit in our constant need to make it significant; though that randomness may serve a larger pattern we are unaware of. Certainly *The Horse and His Boy* is the most "local" and least significant of the Narnia books. Lewis assures us of this by placing it as an interlude in the reigns of the High Kings and Queens, one which was not important enough to be mentioned in *The Lion*. There is, despite surges of excitement in the story, an air of relaxation about this book. Certainly it is the most "novelistic," the most concerned with human relations, of the *Chronicles of Narnia*. Indeed, in some sense it is *about* relaxation, and about freedom, in contrast to *The Silver Chair*, where control was the central theme.

We begin at a critical stage in the life of a boy named Shasta, who has been brought up by a poor fisherman of the land of Calormen, to the south of Narnia. Ill-treated by his adopted father, Shasta is about to be sold into slavery to a passing Tarkaan, or Calormene lord, when he resolves to escape. To his amazement, the Tarkaan's horse speaks to Shasta while his master is inside negotiating his sale, and offers to help him in his journey. For this horse, Bree, is a Narnian Talking Beast, in captivity in Calormen. Both set out to the lands of the north, to Narnia, and on their journey meet a girl, Aravis, on a female talking horse, Hwin. Aravis, a noblewoman, has been promised in marriage to a repulsive old man, Ahoshta, counselor to the ruler of Calormen. She, also, is fleeing north. Their journey takes them via the island city of Tashbaan, where Aravis learns of a Calormene plot to overthrow Archenland, which borders on Narnia and thus threatens Narnia itself. Their subsequent travel across the desert toward Archenland thus takes on added urgency, if they are to forestall the attack led by Prince Rabadash by warning King Lune of Archenland. They succeed, Rabadash is overthrown by an army of Narnian reinforcements as he is besieging King Lune's castle at Anvard, and the threat to Narnia is removed. King Lune recognizes Shasta, who looks identical to his son Corin, as Corin's long-lost elder twin Cor, who was abducted in infancy by a vengeful lord who was also a Calormene spy. Cor and Aravis eventually marry, as do the two talking horses Bree and Hwin, though the latter not to each other.

We can begin with a discussion of what the book is not. The ranging creative imagination that gave us the frozen Narnia of *The Lion, the Witch and the Wardrobe*, the increasingly strange and numinous islands and their inhabitants on the journey to the utter east in *The Voyage of the "Dawn Treader,"* and the ruined city of the giants and Underland in *The Silver Chair*, is not in evidence here. This is not a story of fantastic occurrences or images. The journey in the book could be seen as a secular version of that in *The Voyage of the "Dawn Treader."* There is no supernatural appearance apart from that of Aslan, and he rarely shows himself, except at the end. His role here is not a pervasive one: he simply helps the central characters escape from Calormen, and even this we learn only after the fact.

Lewis gives a special degree of attention in this book to the depiction of a land and its people, and that curiously enough to a land that is not "northern" or Narnian, nor even particularly various or congenial. The book owes a considerable debt to the idiom of James Flecker's *Hassan* (1922), with its rather condescending attitude to the Arabic people,[1] but despite this and the fact that Lewis demonstrates a hostility to the mores of the Calormene race, he has still managed to give us many a vivid thumbnail sketch of a strange country. There is the description of Shasta's first sight of the sea in sunlight, beyond a flower-scattered field ending at a cliff, and beyond that headland after headland (24–25); then the city of Tashbaan, first seen as a mass of lights by night, then by day as an island hill covered with buildings, "terrace above terrace, street above street, zigzag roads or huge flights of steps bordered with orange trees and lemon trees, roof-gardens, balconies, deep archways, pillared colonnades, spires, battlements, minarets, pinnacles" (49); or the strange beehive-shaped tombs of the ancient kings in the desert outside the city, to which Shasta goes at sunset (74). We spend a third of the story in and around the city. As for the Calormene people, there is comedy behind much of the narrative's censure of them; and the moralistic view of the empty-headed, aptly named Lasaraleen, friend to Aravis, who solicits her help in Tashbaan, is muted by what we cannot help but see as her human vitality. "But, darling, only think!," says Lasaraleen, trying to persuade Aravis to marry Ahoshta, now Grand Vizier, "Three palaces, and one of them that beautiful one down on the lake at Ilkeen. Positively ropes of pearls, I'm told. Baths of asses' milk. And you'd see such a lot of me" (88). There is no other of Lewis's Narnia books that spends so much time in the creation of a society of people. In all the others we are aware of some great event impending, some quest in train. We do not know for example that Shasta is actually heir to a throne until late in the narrative. Here there is less pressure because we are simply dealing with two escapees from a particular country. Indeed, at the center of the story is a microsociety composed of Shasta, Aravis, Bree, and Hwin: Shasta, apparently lowborn and humble, beside the at first disdainful Aravis, who has not quite lost her pretensions; the impulsive and vain Bree beside the modest and reserved Hwin. The characters of the horses could be said to play counterpoint to those of their riders. The interrelationships here are seen more at a personal than at a moral level, which is somewhat in contrast, say, to the relationships among the children in *The Lion, the Witch and the Wardrobe* and *The Voyage of the "Dawn Treader."* For instance, neither of those books would have had anything like the episode where Aravis and Bree exchange stories of battles and high life in Calormen, to the discomfiture of Shasta, who knows nothing of such things (43).

Just as we deal with relations among people and horses, so we deal with relations among nations. In Tashbaan, Shasta meets the strange white-skinned humans and the Talking Beasts of the Narnian delegation negotiating Queen Susan's possible marriage to Prince Rabadash. The Narnians mistake him for one of their company, Corin son of King Lune of Archenland, who has gone temporarily missing; Shasta, for his part, as a naturalized Calormene, feels nervous both socially and racially with these people. Then, through the plots of Rabadash and the Tisroc, and through the lands entered by the travelers, we have a growing sense of the proximity and location of Narnia in relation to the lands around it. The Calormenes wish to seize Archenland and Narnia, whether through marriage or war; the Narnians believe in a free community of nations. Insofar as Narnia is the "promised land" toward which the central figures are journeying out of bondage,[2] there is a continued and growing relationship with that place on the part of the travelers. That relationship is as it were sealed when the humble Shasta of Calormen becomes heir to the throne of Archenland, in a way that quite contrasts with the enforced domination planned by the Calormenes. It is curious, too, that in a story where Narnia appears only at the end, it should by the fact that its presence was withheld for so long appear the more real. What this story does is establish another perspective on Narnia, showing it in the context of the countries surrounding it and therefore serving to "thicken" its reality for us.

The story is thus not so ambitious or epic in significance as others of the *Chronicles.* Nevertheless, certain submerged themes thread its narrative, deepening and extending meaning. One of these relates to identity.[3] Shasta, who seems a poor adopted fisherman's boy, is of a white skin that sets him apart from other Calormenes; he is mistaken for the missing Corin by the visiting Narnian party in Tashbaan; and

in the end he is revealed as the long-lost son of King Lune of Archenland. It would be fair to say that his true identity is not simply discovered, but grown into, since Shasta is seen to behave more and more
like a prince throughout the adventure. At first he is the humble and
self-effacing fisher-lad; then he is given accidental and temporary
princedom by the Narnians; and later lives through something of a
dark night of the soul among the tombs, where he must face his terrors.
Thereafter he takes charge in the journey across the desert; helps Aravis
when she is attacked by a lion, and goes forward alone to warn and
secure Narnian help before taking part in the eventual battle at Anvard.
When he is finally recognized as the missing Prince Cor, it is as the
identical twin of Prince Corin. The fact that as the elder son, Shasta/
Cor, now becomes heir to the throne, suggests that his new identity is
as much earned as it is ordained; this is reinforced in the way that
Prince Corin, who would otherwise have been the heir, is content to
stand aside at the claim of his brother.

If those who are humble may find out that they are more than
they seemed, those who are exalted are made humble. This is true of
Aravis, whose insistence on her Calormene station, evident in her
disdain for Shasta, is at odds with her escape from Calormen, defiance
of its laws, and rejection of her birthright. Her accommodation to her
new self is evidenced by her eventual marriage to Shasta/Cor: in the
interim we have seen her take final leave of the society represented by
her friend Lasaraleen, and accept punishment from Aslan for cruelly
leaving her servant-maid to be punished during her initial flight. As
for the vain horse Bree, continually patronizing the female horse Hwin
and bragging about his military exploits in Calormen, he is brought
to a better sense of his true nature when he is overcome by cowardice
and leaves the others at the mercy of a wild lion. The hermit tells him,
"as long as you know you're nobody very special, you'll be a very
decent sort of Horse, on the whole" (129). Bree's nature is never fully
corrected: he remains self-conscious and rather opinionated to the last,
which is a mark of Lewis's realism; and perhaps that is why he never
marries Hwin. The last example of pride in self is Prince Rabadash,
who continues insisting on his "grand" identity, and denying that of
Aslan to the end, when he is literally reduced to an ass. It is a measure

of the confines of his megalomania that he is forbidden by Aslan to go farther than ten miles from Tashbaan, lest his transformation become permanent. He, of course, is only constrained—he learns nothing from his experience.

At the center, metaphysically, of this theme of identity is Aslan himself. As wild lion and cat, he has apparently been present several times throughout the story, though it is not till he is met as himself that we and Shasta learn this. The paradox is that this clearest meeting happens by night, when Shasta finds himself accompanied by an invisible "Thing," which he questions as to its identity, whether it is a giant or a ghost. When told that this thing was the "lions" and the "cat" that variously intervened in his adventure, Shasta asks, "Who *are* you?": " 'Myself,' said the voice, very deep and low so that the earth shook: and again "Myself," loud and clear and gay: and then the third time 'Myself,' whispered so softly you could hardly hear it, and yet it seemed to come from all round you as if the leaves rustled with it" (139–40). This is a reference to the "I am that I am" of Exodus 3:14. Beside this unquestionable self all other selves are contingent, ghosts merely. But this metaphysical nature of identity is used only as a touchstone or yardstick: it does not pervade or alter the story in any great way. So far as Shasta is concerned, his direct meeting with Aslan may represent the finding of his true identity in Christ before a more secular regality is granted him.

We have mentioned that a central concern of the book is with relationship: and certainly there is a growth in true society throughout. Shasta and the fisherman are unrelated in every way; then Shasta and the horse Bree come together to escape; then they are brought together with Aravis and Hwin. "Physical" does not ensure "spiritual" contiguity, however: and this may be symbolized in their long separation from one another in Tashbaan, a city full of people yet almost devoid of true society. The nature of Tashbaan is highlighted by the presence of the Narnians, to whose congenial and genuinely mutual society Shasta is for a time admitted. In Narnian society Talking Beasts and humans live as equals; we hear of few animals in Calormen, apart from horses, which are simply tools of humans there. It is after Tashbaan, in the journey over the desert and the adventures in Archenland, that the

four travelers come closer together and make, as it were, their own
Narnian society. Then Shasta finds that he is part of a larger society,
as heir to Archenland, and not a mere refugee; and Aravis joins him
in marriage.

Yet for all the emphasis on relationship there is an air of solitude
about this story. For much of the time Shasta is on his own, whether
in the initial stages of his journey or as the mistaken Corin in Tashbaan,
or alone for nights at the tombs outside the city, or going on ahead to
warn King Lune, or meeting Aslan by night. And Aravis has left her
own society, though she still tries to cling to its mores; and she finally
quits it when she leaves her erstwhile friend Lasaraleen for the desert.
There is a sense of "singularity" about the story: one fisherman, one
lion, one city, one friend, one cat, one Voice, one castle. Nobody is
told "any story but their own" (139, 170, 174–75). A hermit is the
first person met in Archenland. Loneliness seems pervasive, whether
among the tombs or in the vast emptiness of the desert. There is a
sense of things stripped to their barest essentials; which may suit with
the theme of finding one's true self. For one "message" of the book
appears to be that one cannot relate to others until there is a true
"self" to do the relating. Nevertheless, this does not take away from
the sense that this book is peculiarly spare in details. Perhaps this is
because it is analytic in character: other Narnia books tend to draw
diverse phenomena together, but here we are concerned more with the
natures of the characters and with seeing into them. In a way, it is a
more contemplative book, following a sort of *via negativa* through the
desert, which culminates in Shasta's "dark night of the soul" with
Aslan.

Related to the theme of selfhood is that of freedom, which is
implicitly present throughout the book. At the center of the narrative
are two humans and two horses escaping from a repressive society to
the freedom of Narnia; and the sense of freedom, of course, grows as
they approach their goal. For much of the story, however, we are kept
in Calormen, and, aside from the constant move toward escape by the
central figures, we are taught freedom through the negative mores
of the Calormenes themselves. The Calormenes care nothing for the
identity and separateness of other beings: they seek only to dominate.

The first episode of the book, in which we see how the fisherman Arsheesh has used Shasta, and watch the Tarkaan bid for Shasta's services as a slave, sets the tone. Arsheesh pretends affection for Shasta to heighten his value, a device the Tarkaan sees through, and both treat him as a commodity. Aravis, when first she meets the apparently lowborn Shasta, limits her view of him to his "value" or status in society. In Tashbaan the society is rigidly hierarchical, symbolized by the tiered nature of the city, which improves in elegance as it ascends; and "there is only one traffic regulation, which is that everyone who is less important has to get out of the way for everyone who is more important" (53). In this society marriages are not a matter of choice but of financial and social convenience. It is from this form of slavery that Aravis flees. This kind of Calormene domination is seen also in the veiled threat to the Narnian embassy that, should Queen Susan not agree to marry Prince Rabadash, they will be kept there by force until she does; the Narnians, too, have to make their own prompt escape from Calormen. Parallel to this sexual tyranny is the Calormene urge to subdue other nations by force or fraud. The attack by Rabadash on Archenland is not qualitatively different from his attempt to subjugate Queen Susan to his wishes: the political motive is present in both, the marriage being seen as a way of gaining power in Narnia. Free relationship between individuals seen as equals is almost unknown in Calormen. Even the landscape suggests this: nature is left to wild beasts (there are no Talking Beasts here) or to desert; the people shrink into sparsely scattered communities, symbolized by the island city of Tashbaan, closed in on itself, and compressed into progressively narrower circles as we approach the ruling Tisroc, who sits like an engulfing spider atop this urban cake. This Tisroc, whose affection for his children, as theirs for him, is minimal, is not averse to using his own son as a stalking-horse for an attack on Archenland and Narnia; and announces himself the enemy of "These little barbarian countries that call themselves *free*" (97).

The use of concealment in the manners and speech of the Calormenes is of a piece with this. Their society functions on the hypocritical concealment of rapacity or indifference. The true "self" is suppressed just as everything else: society is composed of a mass of islanded and warring egos, whose only form of communication is through empty eloquence. This leads to inevitably comic effects, as when Arsheesh turns up his rhetoric to sell Shasta to the Tarkaan: "O my master . . . what price could induce your servant, poor though he is, to sell into slavery his only child and his own flesh? Has not one of the poets said, 'Natural affection is stronger than soup and offspring more precious than carbuncles'?" (14). The Calormenes have the habit of reaching for the apt quotation or the proverb: they cite authorities rather than speak for themselves. At the Tisroc's council the Tisroc tries to placate Rabadash's anger at the escape of the Narnians and Queen Susan by resorting to a platitude: "Compose yourself, O my son. . . . For the departure of guests makes a wound that is easily healed in the heart of a judicious host" (95). This apothegm is a rhetorical symbol of the Calormenes: it encapsulates and enslaves truth to mere maxim, it is an islanded linguistic nugget. And in content here it demands the islanding of the self: it proposes that affection be overcome by the judicious mind. Thus words, the apparent cement of society, in Calormen serve only to heighten division, and to further submission and dominance.

This element of concealment pervades all that happens in Calormen. The very fact that Shasta's true race and royal birth are unknown is significant here. Then Shasta and Aravis must continually hide as they try to engineer their escape from Calormen. Even the Narnians must resort to subterfuge, pretending that they are victualing their ship for a great feast to be held with the Calormenes, when they are actually preparing it for departure. They too, it may be noticed, occasionally in this city slip into the aphoristic mode of the Calormenes, though their proverbs are not ornate and are taken from "low" or "beast-fable" contexts (for example, 60, 61). Aslan himself, throughout the journey of the travelers through Calormen, is disguised as a wild lion or a cat; only in Archenland does he reveal himself to Shasta. This concealment motif extends to smaller contexts, as when the unknown Shasta overhears the Narnian plans for escape, or when Aravis and Lasaraleen, hidden behind a sofa in one of the royal rooms, overhear the secret plots of the Tisroc and Rabadash.

Throughout the narrative, as he travels Shasta learns to hide things less. In Tashbaan he is still too much the Calormene to tell the Narnians who he is and reveal Aravis to them: he thinks they would not let him out of the house alive if they knew he was a Calormene, and that for the same reason they would sell Aravis as a slave or send her back to her father (66–67). But outside the city, among the tombs or in the desert, much more exposed, he becomes more open and trusting. (Here we deal with a more inter-personal form of the trust that was asked of the children in *The Silver Chair*.) He is still at first ready to doubt Aravis's faith (75–76); but then he gives himself increasingly to others, whether in guiding his companions across the desert, defending Aravis from the attack of the lion, or going on alone to warn King Lune. After this last journey he finds himself accompanied by night by "One who has waited long for you to speak." He reveals the whole of his history to this Voice, which then in turn identifies itself to him via all the different manifestations of itself it has shown him (138–39). When he has enlisted Narnian help for King Lune, and fought in the battle in defense of Archenland, he can be said to have become fully selfless, and it is at this point that he grows finally into his true self, and King Lune recognizes him as his long-lost son *Cor* (heart).

The societies of Narnia and of Archenland are in marked contrast to that of Calormen. In Narnia, Talking Beasts and men live in varied and equal society: differences are, as it were, "horizontal" between kind and kind, not vertical and hierarchic as they are in Calormen. The very name, "Calor*men*," points to the fact that in that land society is of one species, the human only. There are no cities in Narnia or Archenland, only castles and palaces. Shasta first encounters King Lune while he is out hunting in his countryside, and his initial experience of Narnia is of various Talking Beasts he meets in an area of woodland. These peoples relate to their lands. Nor is there any absorptive center; in Narnia there are four rulers and the king of Archenland shares his regality among his people—when first seen he is simply "a man" mounting a horse among several other gentlemen (131). The relaxed freedom of the Narnians is summed up in their casual dress and manner when Shasta first sees them in Tashbaan (54).

At the center of the book is the journey that Shasta, Aravis, and the two horses have to make not only from Calormen, but from

Calormene ways to those of Narnia. The horses assert and establish themselves as having equal rights with those of the humans. The book is in one way appropriately named *The Horse and His Boy*,[4] for it deliberately inverts the usual relationship, suggesting that dependence works both ways. Increasingly, each member of the party breaks out of his or her egoism or reserve, and learns to relate, to share, and to help. And as they do so, they make up a microcosmic Narnian state of free, democratic, equal, and varied individuals.

Yet the book does not leave us with a sense of freedom as unambiguously valuable. Too much freedom may lead to laxity. When Shasta first meets Talking Beasts in Narnia and warns them of the threat posed to Narnia by Rabadash's attack on King Lune, they all agree that something should be done, but think Calormen too far away to be really galvanized to action: "For the truth was that in the golden age when the Witch and the Winter had gone and Peter the High King ruled at Cair Paravel, the smaller woodland people of Narnia were so safe and happy that they were getting a little careless" (145). Freedom is all very well, but it requires a guard and constant vigilance, or it may be overpowered. But for Shasta, neither King Lune nor the Narnians would have known about Rabadash until it was too late. It is such lack of preparation that the Calormenes are able to exploit with better success in *The Last Battle*.

That freedom is not a good unto itself is also seen in the idea that free choice or even accident are not the sole causes of action in the story. The Voice that comes in the dark to Shasta tells him that it was one and the same with the lion that forced him to join with Aravis, the cat that comforted him among the tombs, the lion that put marauding jackals to flight while he was asleep, and the lion that terrified the horses into increased speed so that Shasta should reach King Lune in time to warn him. And, it adds, "I was the lion you do not remember who pushed the boat in which you lay, a child near death, so that it came to shore where a man sat, wakeful at midnight, to receive you" (139). Later still the lion is to tell Aravis that it was he who tore her with his claws, for they equaled the lashes given to the slave-maiden of her stepmother's whom Aravis indifferently drugged in order to make her first escape (169). In the face of this we may begin to wonder at certain other events in the story. Why did the Tarkaan come when he did, and on a Narnian talking horse with an urge to escape like Shasta's? How was it that by "the merest accident" Aravis and Lasaraleen should conceal themselves in the very room where the Tisroc, the Vizier, and Rabadash would discuss their secret plot against Archenland and Narnia? And of course we know that the recalcitrant horse and the mist that eventually separate Shasta from King Lune's party put him on the way to warn the Narnians and bring reinforcements. Acts of free choice obviously have their place: the courage to change one's life, to escape, to endure dangers, terrors, and a difficult journey, to act on behalf of others, to go on alone when it seems pointless. But in the larger scheme of things now presented, each free act makes up part of a providential pattern, each apparent piece of chance is a piece of the divine plan. In the end Shasta/Cor turns out to have fulfilled a prophecy made long ago at his birth by a Centaur-seer, who declared, "A day will come when that boy will save Archenland from the deadliest danger in which ever she lay" (173). And the hermit tells Aravis, "I have now lived a hundred and nine winters in this world and have never yet met any such thing as Luck" (126). Here we see another possible form of the idea of relationship celebrated in the book, for here mortal acts of choice and ultimately divine providence can be seen as joined together to produce a happy outcome—an outcome in which the continuance of free choice itself, imaged in the lands of Narnia and Archenland, is alone assured. Interestingly, these providential moments and patterns are revealed only near the end of the narrative, and have to be applied retrospectively to acts we have previously taken at face value as chance or free choice. But that could be just the point.

# 10

## *The Magician's Nephew*

In this book Lewis describes the creation of Narnia by Aslan, who is assisted by certain human arrivals. Since hundreds of years may pass in Narnia without any time lapsing in England, Lewis could have set Narnia's origins at some point in time quite close to the wartime exploration of it by the children of *The Lion, the Witch and the Wardrobe*, but he chose to place it "contemporary" with the Edwardian world of his own childhood. This gives the book a certain authenticity and verve;[1] numbers of readers have found his presentation of children in the other books rather dated, more an adult's view of how a child growing up in the 1940s and 1950s should be than how children naturally are. The story contradicts the declaration in *The Lion* that Peter, Susan, Edmund, and Lucy are the first Sons of Adam and Daughters of Eve to enter Narnia. In *The Magician's Nephew* we see the establishment of a line of human kings and queens upon its creation.

In a sense this is an explanatory book. How did the witch first get into Narnia? What about the lamppost? How did Narnia begin? Lewis is partly tying up loose ends, finding reasons for things he was earlier prepared to leave unexplained. In fact, he began writing a book with this aim in view directly after *The Lion*: Roger Lancelyn Green, his friend, described how Lewis showed him a fragment in June 1949 that featured Polly, Digory, and a helpful fairy-godmother figure called Mrs. Lefay, but this was set aside as unsatisfactory. Again in May 1951 Lewis got as far as a story including Charn, but it contained a too-lengthy account of a rustic named Piers and his wife, who were to become the first king and queen of Narnia. On Green's advice, this episode was deleted and *The Magician's Nephew* as we have it completed by February 1954.[2]

Yet despite Lewis's concern with its origins, Narnia is far from central to *The Magician's Nephew*. We do not reach it until precisely halfway through the book, and even then have to wait a further two chapters until it is identified as Narnia. The children in this story, having no connection with those in the others, have no idea of where they might be, nor do they recognize the singing lion that makes the world as Aslan. Only one paragraph at the beginning of the book—"This is a story about something that happened long ago when your grandfather was a child. It is a very important story because it shows how all the comings and goings between our own world and the land of Narnia first began"—places us within a Narnia context, and it is one that for long in the story we may lose sight of. Indeed, Narnia has begun to play a somewhat less central part in the stories after *The Lion* and *Prince Caspian*, even if our sense of it is widened by traveling beyond its frontiers. In *The Voyage of the "Dawn Treader"* we are on a Narnian ship exploring other lands and islands far to the east; in *The Silver Chair* most of the action takes place beyond Narnia or underground; and in *The Horse and His Boy*, while Narnia is the ultimate destination of the travelers, most of the narrative is set in Calormen and, later, in Archenland. And if, in *The Horse and His Boy*, Narnia was described geographically as one among a number of other actual lands, here its existence is contingent, created out of nothing, and seen as one among a number of *possible* and alternative worlds—whether of Charn, or Edwardian London, or any of the other places that might have been reached via the many magic pools from the "in-between" place (to all of which we shall come). So, paradoxically, despite the book's being "about" the creation of Narnia, the presence of Narnia itself is relatively muted. The very fullness with which it is eventually brought into being is as it were surrounded by other possibilities.

This is reinforced by the nondirectional style of the narrative. In all the other stories some overriding purpose soon becomes evident, whether it is the saving of Narnia from a witch or a usurper, a voyage to the utter east, a quest for a lost prince, an escape to Narnia through hostile territory, or an attempted rescue of Narnia from ruin. Only in *The Last Battle* does a different kind of narrative appear, that of the final destruction of Narnia by Aslan, beyond its local devastation by Calormene invaders and erosion through internal dissent. But that narrative is predicated on the others, and there is certainly a clear single purpose throughout. In *The Magician's Nephew* everything is much more compartmentalized. The child characters are tricked by their evil uncle Andrew into putting on rings that transport them out of this world. He gives them a means of return, for he simply wants to know where they will go. And where they go is not to Narnia but to a strange, silent, wooded place filled with pools, where they have largely forgotten their world and who they were in it. When after a number of separate adventures they reach Narnia, it is via one of the pools in this wood, chosen at random. Nothing, so far as the reader is concerned, has led up to this, though from the standpoint of divine providence all may be part of a larger pattern invisible to mortals.

The story describes how two Edwardian children, Digory Kirke and Polly Plummer, are sent out of this world into some other by their uncle. The children discover the principles governing the magic rings that transported them, but rather than return directly, they enter a dying world called Charn, where they inadvertently bring to life the statue of a beautiful but cruel woman. She is Jadis, destroyer of Charn, who is to be the evil White Witch of Narnia. Despite their efforts to evade her, the children unwittingly bring her with them to London, where she wreaks havoc, before they are successful in using Uncle Andrew's magic rings to take her into another world. This world proves at first to be quite dark and rocky; but soon there is singing, stars come out, grass and trees cover the land, and then all manner of creatures, including Talking Beasts, are created by a wondrous lion. The witch flings an ineffectual missile at the lion and makes off on her own.

Thus Narnia is born. A cabdriver named Frank, who has accidentally been brought into the new world along with the children, is made king, and his wife, brought at the call of the lion, is crowned queen with him. Then Digory is given a task. He must journey to the mountains beyond Narnia and locate a lake in a valley, beside which is a green mound with a garden crowning it. Within the garden he will find a tree loaded with apples. He must return to Aslan with one of these apples, whereupon it will be planted in the Narnian mud and the tree that grows from it will keep the witch a hundred miles distant from it so long as it lives. This journey Digory accomplishes on the back of the cabbie's horse, which has been given wings by Aslan. Inside the garden, he is tempted to eat the apple he plucks, but resists; the witch tempts him to use it to bring his sick mother at home back to health, and this temptation is far harder for him to overcome. He chooses to obey Aslan and return to Narnia, and in the end is given a fruit from the new tree that genuinely heals his mother in a way a stolen one never would have.

Perhaps the nearest in spirit of the Narnia books to this one is the first, *The Lion, the Witch and the Wardrobe*, and perhaps not inappropriately so, since *The Lion* marks the beginning of the *Chronicles* and this book marks the beginning of Narnia itself. One of the motifs in *The Lion* is that of growth: spring comes to long-frozen Narnia and all come alive again. Further, the seeming accident by which the children entered Narnia in *The Lion* grew into a larger divine plan; and the magic at work became progressively deeper. Growth is of course central to the idea of creation in *The Magician's Nephew*. As the title "*The Lion, the Witch and the Wardrobe*" brings together three apparently separate motifs or story lines into a unity, so in *The Magician's Nephew* there is a similar binding together of diverse elements, though they are still more various here. In *The Lion* all the separate items related to Narnia; but in *The Magician's Nephew* we spend time in three quite different worlds—four, if one counts the magic pools in the "in-between" world: Edwardian London, the urbanized ruin of Charn, and the strange dark place that becomes the pastoral world of Narnia. That Lewis has managed to join such different places together into a convincing unity shows him as artist imitating, or, as he might accept participating in, the creative power of Aslan, who can make a world capacious enough to sustain, in living harmony, Talking Beasts, a London cabbie, an Edwardian lamppost, and a toffee-tree.

Nevertheless, *The Magician's Nephew* is distinctive in its restlessness, even in relation to *The Voyage of the "Dawn Treader,"* for there, even if the ship was continually moving from island to island, it had a constant direction, toward the utter east and ultimately Aslan's country. Here there is recurrent shifting from place to place, for a long stretch without evident purpose. The children travel to the strange "in-between" world, then go to Charn, wake up Jadis and unwittingly transport her to London, after which a whole series of bizarre clashes of culture occur. The children eventually succeed in getting her out of their world, once again into the in-between world, and thence to Narnia. The continual element of surprise in this, of being abruptly shifted from one world to another, reinforces the ideas of creation and awakening that become the themes of the book when it reaches Narnia. But the way in which we can never anticipate what is going to happen next, never be sure or familiar enough of the ground rules of the story to form suppositions from them, gives a strange contingency to the narrative. This is added to by the way that the character of one world is played against another: the hard, dead, urbanized world of Charn at the end of its time, against the mobile, pliant, pastoral world of Narnia at the beginning of its history. Again, *Charn,* which shares some of the letters of *Narnia,* has few perspectives, and is an enclosed world of buildings; where Narnia is much more open, and almost the first thing Digory does when he gets there is to travel to its end and beyond it to the mountains.

This contingency ultimately relates to Narnia, which shimmers into being out of darkness. Indeed here *The Magician's Nephew* and *The Last Battle* have much in common—for in the one Narnia is created out of nothing, and in the other it is returned to nothing. It is, as it were, no longer ontologically secure. In the books up to now our sense of it has been steadily thickened, first through the thorough exploration of it in *The Lion, the Witch and the Wardrobe* and *Prince Caspian,* then indirectly, through the journeys to its environs in *The Voyage of the "Dawn Treader," The Silver Chair,* and *The Horse and*

*His Boy*. But now, as we approach the end of the *Chronicles* and find the beginning and the end of Narnia in the two final novels, the place begins to fade, and even as its inception is described, we feel the pressure of the darkness all about it, not to mention the reality of the alternative worlds in the book that we have visited before we come to this one.

Peculiar to this novel and to *The Last Battle* is a sense whereby the boundaries of things are indistinct. Children from Edwardian London enter and affect Charn; and by the same token, a leading representative of that world enters London—and all enter Narnia. No place is impermeable. And all worlds come together in a sense as a series of pools in the in-between world of the wood. Further, objects from one world may enter and find different use or life in another. In the wood, Polly and Digory comes across the experimental guinea pig Uncle Andrew sent out of this world. The empress Jadis comes to London in her splendidly barbaric clothes. A cab-horse or a piece of lamppost enter Narnia and are transformed.

Adding to the sense of insecurity is the element of the apparently accidental in the plot. Of course it is a favorite device of Lewis's to show that all seemingly random acts are part of a larger design, as he does with the children's "chance" entry into Narnia in *The Lion, the Witch and the Wardobe*, or with the wild beasts in *The Horse and His Boy*, which turn out to be Aslan in disguise. But even in *The Horse and His Boy* we were given so much scope to think events "chance" or ordinary, as to make it harder for us later to accept that they were, from the first, part of a larger providential action. In *The Magician's Nephew* acts are allowed to stray still more widely before being corralled within sense or "design." As has already been discussed, we do not reach what is to be Narnia until halfway through the book, and nothing has anticipated our arrival in such a place apart from the introductory paragraph to the novel.

The book begins with Polly and Digory exploring the linked attics of their houses when they happen on the garret study of Uncle Andrew. He is just at the point in his magical researches of requiring human subjects for his experiments with magic rings. The rings that take the children out of this world put them in what turns out to be a magical jumping-off place between many worlds, the silent wood full of pools, to step into any of which is to be transported to a wholly different "other" world. This means, when they think of it, that they have to mark the pool from which they emerged, to be sure of returning to their own world. The place operates by chance for them, since they have no way of telling where any pool will take them. The one they eventually jump into takes them to a place they would not have chosen, the land of Charn, a ruined, citified world beneath a dying red sun. Once in this world, they wander at random through streets, courtyards, and buildings until they come upon a hall filled with a line of seated figures. These figures look alive, but are immobile. On a table in the center of the hall is a little hanging bell and a hammer, and a verse daring its reader to "*Make your choice, adventurous Stranger; / Strike the bell and bide the danger, / Or wonder, till it drives you mad, / What would have followed if you had*" (50). We are clearly meant to understand that Digory does wrong in obeying this, but there is no means by which he (or we) could have known the consequences: namely that at the sound of the bell the last and most evil-looking individual in the line of seated figures will come awake and eventually follow the children into Narnia as the White Witch, later putting that world into endless winter and killing Aslan.

By the frailest-seeming chance, the witch (at present, known to us as the Empress Jadis), is able to return with the children to London. They seemed to have shaken her off in Charn when they put on their rings to go back to the wood between worlds, only to find that she was able to accompany them by virtue of her grasp on Polly's hair, for the rings work on all bodies with which they are in contact, directly or indirectly. The same happens on the trip back to London, when last-minute sympathy for her on Digory's part allows the witch to catch hold of his ear between her finger and thumb. Now clearly we can read this on a different level, in terms of the children having an element of the witch within themselves that gives her a handhold on them. But there is still the overriding sense of events occurring by chance that imbues the narrative with a feeling of "If only. . . ."

Similar "chance" governs the journey to Narnia. Digory's choice and will get the witch out of London, but he did not expect, when he arrived with her and Polly in the wood, to find Uncle Andrew, the hansom cabdriver Frank, and a cab-horse also of the party. And it is no human choice that leads to the next pool they enter: had it been (one is to suppose), the children would have taken Jadis back to Charn. Instead it is the cab-horse, wandering off in search of a drink, who pulls them all with it into a quite unexpected world. And at a quite unexpected time in the history of this world. For it appears that the arrival of the motley group coincides with its creation. We may suppose if we will that Narnia was "timed" by Aslan to begin with their arrival, but that only throws into sharper relief his use of apparent accident as the trigger for this.

Thereafter, of course, under the aegis of Aslan, everything becomes part of a plan. The wrenched-off piece of a London lamppost that Jadis is still carrying as a weapon is turned, after she has thrown it in vain at the lion who is making the world, into a new lamppost in the soil of Narnia: and this is the lantern that Lucy sees on her first arrival in Narnia in *The Lion, the Witch and the Wardrobe*. The witch, who then flees, is to become the great evil of Narnia. The making of the cabdriver and his wife into the first king and queen of Narnia, and the use of Digory and of the cab-horse to secure an apple from a tree in a far garden that will grow to be a tree of protective life for Narnia, shows the use of apparently chance materials by Aslan to further a grand design. Yet while all this is true, and while in a real sense seeming chance may be said, in a manner peculiarly appropriate to this book, to *grow* into a divine scheme, there is still the interplay of plan against ostensible planlessness in the two halves of the book: and this adds to our sense of evanescence, of the uncertain status of any phenomenon, as though each could either come to be or cease to be in an instant.

The motif of growth, as stated earlier, is not peculiar to this book—it is also present in *The Lion, the Witch and the Wardrobe*—but it is most marked here, and can be seen in almost every aspect of the book. For instance, in the use of magic. Uncle Andrew is a mere meddler who has got hold of an Atlantean dust that enables travel out of this world, but he has neither the vision nor the courage to attempt the journey himself. His magic rings nevertheless work in tandem with the pools to take the children to Charn, where the bell awakens Jadis.

# The Magician's Nephew

The magic of Jadis is far more potent than anything yet seen in the book and belittles Uncle Andrew's. But when the children reach Narnia, they find a deeper magic at work, the magic of a lion's song that fills a sky with stars, makes a sun to light a world, and covers that world with wood and grass and water, and populates it with a variety of living creatures, including some made rational. And beyond even that, there is a still deeper magic: and that is the magic of free choice, by which Aslan allows his creatures to help or hinder his own grand design. The resistance of Digory to temptation is seen to be in a sense a far greater wizardry than Uncle Andrew's. It is here perhaps that we are most reminded of the deepening magic seen in *The Lion, the Witch and the Wardrobe* and in *The Voyage of the "Dawn Treader."*

The children are seen to demonstrate a growth in understanding. At first they simply stumble on their adventures, the dupes of Uncle Andrew. Increasingly they learn the properties of the magic rings: the yellow ones take one to the wood of pools, and the green ones enable one to travel to another world from that wood. More than this, the children come to see the consequences of their actions. Unlike Uncle Andrew, who is concerned only with personal gain, and can, for instance, only see the witch as "A dem fine woman, sir, a dem fine woman" (73), they see the results of idle curiosity and thoughtless experiment, starting with the release of Jadis through Digory's striking the bell, moving on through their attempts to shake her off, and then to their more altruistic endeavour to remove her dangerous presence from their London world. By the end Digory can see through the deceptions of the witch when she tempts him to misuse the apple, showing that he has gained full control over himself and his life, even while he submits both to Aslan's will.

This growth in understanding is moral too. At first the children are curious. No harm in that, one might think, but curiosity is associated with magic and with Uncle Andrew. It is perhaps fitting that they stumble on his study when exploring the attics (oddly, they have counted the rafters and think they are well past Digory's house). Polly is attracted by the rings and readily puts one on, and thus vanishes. Digory has the goodness to risk all to go to rescue her. Nevertheless, when he finds her, he persuades her to enter another world; and once they are in Charn he will not turn back, despite her fears of the place. It is he who strikes the bell. A trivial act, one might again suppose; but one that like every other expands beyond all bounds, just as the tiny bell grows to a great booming sound. One act of "original sin" spreads out to embrace whole worlds, and it is the children who are to take the witch, who as we have said is perhaps symbolically a part of them in being attached to them, into Narnia. That act is to be answered by one that symbolically reverses the Fall of Man itself, in Digory's taking one apple from the tree in the garden and refusing to use it for himself, but rather for the health of the whole world of Narnia. He has learned to do without self, and without trying to manipulate reality for his own sake. In this he and Polly are the direct opposite of the witch, who thereby does not grow but declines, from an impressive and morally ambiguous stature as the Empress Jadis, to the mere hater of all good that she appears in Narnia.

In parallel with this there is a decline in the use of magical apparatus in the story, as the children grow closer to their true selves. The rings, and learning the rules by which they operate, at first dominate; as does the magical bell that wakens Jadis. But in Narnia magic is much more direct, coming from the creative power of a lion's song. At the same time, the story almost literally opens out. We start in narrow places, in attics, Uncle Andrew's study, in the buildings of Charn, in the urban world of London, even in the rather claustrophobic wood between worlds: but then in Narnia distances open out (and Digory has to travel them). Once he has returned home, Digory's restored family move out from London to the country. A third element accompanying the "growth" motif is that of increase in society; here we come close again to the idiom of *The Lion, the Witch and the Wardrobe*. As the children move through the story they draw into their adventure more people—even the cab-horse Strawberry—and by the time they reach Narnia they find themselves in the midst of a new society being created. It is that society for which Digory acts, while the witch—and this is the measure of her nature—goes off alone; she was alone in a similar way in being the only individual wakened from the line of people by Digory's striking the bell. Uncle Andrew, we may notice, is also estranged from the Narnian creatures, whose speech he cannot understand, but he at least is still made to be "social" by them, in that he is in the center of their to him unwelcome though well-meant attentions. He may be in a cage, symbol of his self-enclosure, but he is also the focus of uncomprehending charity. And the result is that he partly reforms.

One of the motifs of the book is communication. This is symbolized in the way that worlds are interconnected through the "telephone exchange" of the wood with its magic pools; even, too, in the unexpected linkage of all the roof spaces in the row of London houses at the start. Words here are significant. Uncle Andrew and the witch use them to lie, and Andrew thus becomes incomprehensible in Narnia. The destroying force of the witch's "Deplorable Word" in one world is countered by the creative power of the lion's song in another. The power of the witch's evil spells is largely lost in our world; and wholly so in the presence of Aslan in Narnia. And the culminating point of Aslan's creation of Narnia is to make beasts into Talking Beasts.

In this book of all the Narnia books we are most aware of children in relation to adults. One of the implicit ideas in the book is what it means to be truly "adult" and what it means to be "childish." The children grow spiritually without ceasing to be children—it is that kind of child that Christ came to save. But the adult Uncle Andrew is inside morally childish and regressive. As for the cabdriver Frank and his wife Helen, they grow back to their true country selves, into child-like innocence. The witch, of course, has no part in spiritual or natural biology. She is stasis, and she will stop Narnia's growth later by freezing it to continual winter. She destroys worlds, where the lion makes them. She comes from a land of death and stone—Narnia's obverse, Charn.

Yet growth reminds us also of mortality. The Narnia that is now created in all freshness is subject to change, which will only for a time be kept at bay by the tree grown from Digory's apple. Digory's mother has a terminal illness from which only grace-given magic can save her. Digory will become the white-bearded Professor Kirke who is host to the children in *The Lion, the Witch and the Wardrobe*. If growth signifies the new, and the idea of evolution, it also contains the idea of evolution and endings. In that sense *The Magician's Nephew* grows naturally into *The Last Battle*.

There remain certain kinds of growth that have little to do with time and belong to deeper laws. There is, for example, the idea of something large being made out of something small or apparently insignificant—the choice of a ring, the curiosity that causes a bell to be struck, the swelling sound of a tiny bell, the power of one apple from the tree in the garden to the west of Narnia. Disproportion, if we may thus term it, is at the heart of Christianity, whether for good or ill: out of one apple eaten comes all mankind's evil; out of one death comes the redemption of humanity. And there is another principle, a law whereby out of evil, good always emerges. For all his bumbling greed, Uncle Andrew sets in motion a process that culminates in the making of Narnia. The broken-off piece of a lamppost that the witch uses as a weapon against Aslan grows into a lantern that will light the way into Narnia for its later human saviors. Out of the death of Charn comes the creation of Narnia. Out of a cabdriver and his wife come the first king and queen of Narnia. Out of dumb animals come rational Talking Beasts; out of a cab-horse is made a Pegasus; out of an apple got in obedience comes a whole tree to preserve Narnia. As the Oyér-esu, or guardian intelligences of Mars and Venus, sing at the end of Lewis's *Perelandra*, the story of an averted fall on another planet, "After earths, not better earths but beasts; after beasts, not better beasts but spirits. After a falling, not recovery but a new creation. Out of the new creation, not a third but the mode of change itself is changed itself."[3]

# 11

## The Last Battle

This is the book that sees the ending of Narnia; though also, in a further sense, its beginning. Narnia is invaded by Calormenes (what threatened in *The Horse and His Boy*). Narnia's king, Tirian, proves helpless against the invaders, and sees his subjects enslaved. The story begins, however, on the margins of Narnia, with seemingly peripheral creatures and events. A Narnian talking ape called Shift has dressed up a simple donkey, Puzzle, in a wild lion's skin to look like Aslan, who has long been absent from Narnia. With this "Aslan," whom Shift usually keeps concealed in a stable, he gains considerable power over the Narnians, who believe he speaks with Aslan's authority. Shift aligns himself with the Calormenes, but he is besotted with his power, and more subtle minds than his are at work to use him in turn as their tool. Tirian secures the help of the children Eustace Scrubb and Jill Pole, who arrive from England, and they uncover the fraud and capture the donkey disguised as Aslan. Yet through the cunning of their enemies the Narnians are persuaded that Aslan continues to inhabit the stable, though now disdaining to reveal himself. Both Shift and the other plotters have no belief in the reality either of Aslan or of the god of the Calormenes, the hideous Tash. But the ape, even if in disbelief, has at one point called on Tash; and, unknown to them all, Tash has come and entered the stable. Behind the evil vision of the divine that is Tash, is Aslan. Thus there are layers within layers, and each who seems in charge is in the control of a larger power. In the end Tirian and the children are defeated and forced into the stable. Then Aslan comes, and with him the last judgment of all the creatures of Narnia and its surrounding countries, followed by the destruction of their world. Those who pass through Aslan's great doorway enter a beautiful new country, the environs of heaven; and there they meet with the children from other Narnia stories.

This is a book of contrasts, between the noble and the sordid, between the horrifying (Tash) and the glorious (Aslan). The book begins with the ape's seamy manipulations of the donkey and his gradual formulation of a cheap plot to impersonate Aslan; it ends with the wonder of Aslan's country. The threat to Narnia is evident in the Calormenes' felling of the talking trees of Narnia and oppression of the talking horses, said to be sanctioned by Aslan. There is always the sense of what Narnia was, and what it is becoming. At one point the children and Tirian are shown at sunrise, with the dew glistening and the birds singing, but we know as they do that all this is under threat. The center of attention in Narnia is here not its king nor its palace of Cair Paravel, but a crude stable that houses a fraudulent god. And that image contrasts in our minds with the biblical image of the manger of Bethlehem, an image of authenticity. The Calormene's Tash is a god with the stench of death, "roughly the shape of a man but . . . [with] the head of a bird; some bird of prey with a cruel, curved beak" (76); the contrast between this horror and Aslan puts in final and divine terms the clash between falsity and truth, corruption and innocence, death and life, that runs through out the book.

The fact that we start with so petty a creature as the ape and so clumsy a scheme ably serves this contrast. The way the donkey, aptly named Puzzle, is so continually the dupe of Shift, anticipates the Narnians' gullibility at the hands of the ape, the ease with which they are deceived. There is also a sense of disproportion in the casual locality with which the story begins, with this tramplike ape and his companion. It is hard to believe that such a pair and such a plot are able to undermine all Narnia. That they are successful suggests something not so much about them as about the condition of Narnia itself.[1]

On the surface, all seems much like earlier incidents, say, the incursions of the White Witch and the hundred years' winter in the first book of the *Chronicles*. Aslan has been away for a long time and the Narnians have forgotten what he looks like. Tirian the king, with his loyal friends, Jewel the unicorn, Roonwit the centaur, and Farsight the eagle, seems as noble and straightforward as, say, Caspian in the second and third Narnia books. Can one blame the Narnians for being tricked into believing in the ape's false Aslan and his dictates, or for submitting to the Calormene invaders because they think it is the will of their god? Can one blame Tirian for the eventual loss of Cair Paravel and thus of all Narnia to the invading Calormene fleet when he could not have foreseen the treachery of Shift? Do not matters seem still more out of his hands when Roonwit explains that Narnia's doom is written in a rare and portentous conjunction of the stars? (19–20)

And yet, we feel that something is lacking in these Narnians in "the last days" of their world. The king is at the outset enjoying himself at his hunting lodge: thereafter, he is continually wandering or helpless. Instead of being the center, or being *at* the center, he is on the periphery. The focus of Narnia is the ape and the hut of the false Aslan. Tirian's behavior at the start is impractical and ill thought out. Enraged by the slaughter of Narnian talking trees, he sets off with only Jewel to challenge the Calormenes; and once he finds them is so much further incensed at the fact that they are using a Narnian talking horse to drag timber that he and Jewel kill two of them. They flee the scene, but Tirian's fear that he has gone against Aslan's will compels them to return and surrender to the Calormenes. Later, when he has again escaped and has Eustace and Jill to help him, Tirian resolves on a scheme to rescue Jewel. But it is Jill who thinks to investigate "Aslan" in the nearby hut, Jill who uncovers the fraud perpetrated by Shift and returns with the pathetic Puzzle she finds this "Aslan" to be. Tirian thinks locally and is thus marginalized.

This is true also of his erstwhile subjects. They, too, are on the periphery, whether as slaves to the Calormenes or as dupes of the ape. Many of them so believe the ape that they are prepared to fight against their king. Puzzlement characterizes the best of them, and of course Aslan has become for them a Puzzle. They are continually outwitted, by the ape, the cat Ginger, or Rishda Tarkaan the Calormene. This helplessness, this marginalization, this readiness to believe the false, in the end says something about *them* at least as much as about their oppressors. These disorganized, bemused figures are not those we saw in the prime of Narnia. They have in a sense devolved, been diminished. Perhaps that is why *dwarfs* and their poverty of attitude are so present in this book (though the dwarfs here are foolish cynics, the apparent opposite of dupes). The ape, by contrast, claims to be a man: in a reversal of Darwin he says that he is so old and wise a man that he has come to look like an ape; it is the rest who are "a lot of stupid animals" (32). Indeed, to a large extent the Narnian Talking Beasts are bereft of the intelligence that distinguished them from mere brutes. Increasingly they are referred to collectively as "beasts." When seen from the ape's vantage point by night outside the hut they appear as "dozens of eyes shining with the reflection of the fire, as you've seen a rabbit's or a cat's eyes in the headlights of a car" (91): this image "dehumanizes" the Talking Beasts and reduces them to dumb animals. We are not too far from Wells's *The Island of Dr. Moreau* here.

Other Narnia books dealt with the theme of growing into or finding one's identity: this book deals with the loss of that identity. Where in previous books as much force of imagery went into the depiction of the "good" as of the evil—we think of Mrs. Badger, the High King Peter, Caspian, Puddleglum, Reepicheep, Shasta, or Digory—here Lewis's descriptive powers center on the ape in his absurd red jacket and crown (image of the whore of Babylon?), the cynical dwarves, the supersubtle cat, and finally the horror that is Tash. Even Aslan's image is perverted as Puzzle dons the lion skin. The ape is rightly called Shift: he twists reality; he attempts even to shift out of his own nature. Narnia is steadily ceasing to be Narnia, invaded by Calormenes, its Talking Beasts reduced to mere beasts, its animate trees to timber, its king to a largely unacknowledged partisan. Aslan is "merged" with Tash by the plotters to become "Tashlan." When Tirian summons the former helpers of Narnia in his hour of need, he can only appear to them as a speechless and quickly fading phantom. He loses his crown early on. When Eustace and Jill arrive in Narnia, they are uncertain how they got there: later they find they were killed in a train wreck.

Disguise plays an important role—one thinks of Puzzle's lion skin and the Calormene armor and face paint used by Tirian and the children. The imagery of clothing is recurrent, with the implication that reality can be masked or perverted. (*Shift* can also refer to a piece of clothing.) The ape gives the crowd glimpses of Puzzle's "Aslan" at night; this is described as a sort of theater (93). And here more than in any other book of the *Chronicles*, actions take place by night, not least because concealment is always of the essence. The book is concerned with those who are trying and failing to find out the truth, and those who are successfully concealing the truth. This is a book largely of plots and schemes the object of which is to gain or maintain power. It is, *pace Prince Caspian*, the most purely political of the Narnia books, involved as it is with assertion and counterassertion in state matters. And in the middle of this is uncertain identity. Is Aslan in the hut? If he is not, is the hut empty? We think the latter to be the case, but we are proved wrong. Rishda Tarkaan and Ginger the cat believe neither Tash nor Aslan inhabit the structure, but they are wrong. The truth lies "farther up and farther in," and is found at the end of a contest over what is the true being of a thing.

In a sense the book is a kind of exercise in analysis. If not that, then what? But it is also a reductive analysis. The ape removes certainty from the very basis of reality on which Narnia is founded, when he defrauds the nature of Aslan. He takes away the keystone of the whole structure of the world by putting the false in place of the true and having it worshiped by the Narnians. The Narnians are diminished when they worship that which does not accord with the nature of Aslan as they have been taught it. More directly, Shift inadvertently begins the destruction of Narnia that is announced in the stars: he lets the Calormenes in, and permits the destruction of holy trees and the enslavement of Narnians. He announces these things to be the orders of Aslan himself (23–24): and in a sense he speaks far truer than he knows; as does Tirian when, in answer to Jewel's question, "But, Sire, how *could* Aslan be commanding such dreadful things?" he replies,

"He is not a *tame* Lion. . . . How should we know what he would do?" (28). The ape and the other evil characters are, in effect, mere tools of Aslan: in allowing Narnia to be overrun, its king dethroned, its people made captive, and its landscape ravaged, they are preparing the way for the final destruction that is in store for it, when Aslan truly comes to it, and for the last time. Then its being is finally unraveled in the fall of the stars, the devouring of its verdure by huge monsters, its engulfment by a giant wave, and the crushing of its sun into the final night anticipated by all the other night scenes in the book.

But this is not all. After the end of things there is a new beginning. In the death of Narnia lies the reality of Aslan: and in that reality Narnia grows rather than diminishes. When the children have gone through the stable door, and have witnessed the ending of Narnia behind them, they find themselves in a land that seems increasingly familiar, until at last they realize that it is a larger and somehow much more real Narnia. The Lord Digory whom they meet there tells them that they are in "Aslan's real world," and in that world, "All of the old Narnia that mattered, all the dear creatures, have been drawn into the real Narnia through the Door" (154). And they go "farther up and farther in." They travel through and beyond this Narnia till they come to a hilltop garden amid the mountains, in the "same" place that Digory found it in *The Magician's Nephew* when he went to fetch an apple, and there they see that the garden is really a whole world, a further Narnia, "more real and more beautiful than the Narnia down below, just as *it* was more real and more beautiful than the Narnia outside the Stable door" (162–63). In this world things get not less, but progressively more real. Where previously we had a loss of identity to the point of total annihilation, now we have the realization of selfhood beyond all imagining. In a sense—though only in a sense—the old Narnia is to this world what the pretense of Aslan was to the truth. Inasmuch as the ape's fraudulent schemes the ("aping" of reality) could be said to have led to the truth of Aslan, so is the narrative as a whole in relation to the world in which those schemes once operated. In that larger pattern, the locality of the earlier action at Caldron Pool and the hut yields to the ever-dilating cosmic and yet human reality of Aslan. And what was a theater designed to falsify becomes a platform for truth.

The book is clearly divided between what happens in front of the stable door, and what happens in the "supernatural" world beyond it. Before it, all life has converged. Certainly events literally narrow down to the door as focus. At first we may visit other parts of Narnia, but gradually the hut becomes the center of interest; and in the end Tirian and his followers are trapped there and killed or thrown through the door. Then the door becomes the focus for the departure of all creatures from that world, and their final judgment. But thereafter what has converged now expands outward into wider and still wider reality. The inside of the stable seems, to those with spiritual vision, bigger than all that is outside: and Queen Lucy sounds the first note of this expanding reality, "In our world too, a stable once had something inside it that was bigger than our whole world" (128).

At first the truth is always hidden inside things—inside the lion skin that covers Puzzle, inside the hut, inside the head of the ape. We deal much with enclosures, down to the damp and almost windowless tower in which Tirian seeks refuge. Each scheme moves, as it were, farther in as new lies must be fabricated to explain the disappearance of Tirian from captivity, or of "Aslan" from the hut. The process is one of moving through the layers of these schemes to the truth that is finally revealed at their center.[2] But on the other side of the door, the process is reversed. We moved from "enclosures" outward. What seems small is always expanding. We seem to travel into more confined places, from the old Narnia to the limits of the stable, and from the new Narnia to the little circle of the garden at its edge: but each of these proves to hold a world far larger than the one before. As Mr. Tumnus the faun (of *The Lion, the Witch and the Wardrobe*), puts it "The farther up and the farther in you go, the bigger everything gets. The inside is larger than the outside"; and when Queen Lucy wonders at the increasing reality of the series of new Narnias they pass through, with "world within world, Narnia within Narnia," the faun replies, "Yes . . . like an onion: except that as you go in and in, each circle is larger than the last" (162, 163).

The larger idiom of the book is paradox and reversal. In trying to perpetrate a lie, the ape and the others "call down" ultimate truth. By setting a false god in a stable, the ape serves to put a true one there. The commandment ceaselessly violated here is, "Thou shalt not take the name of the Lord thy God in vain" (Exodus 20.7); and the reference is also to the false Christs of the last days described in Matthew 24. In destroying Narnia, Aslan makes it far more real. What seemed annihilation becomes the way to fuller life. What began with a discarded lion skin washed down the waterfall at Caldron Pool, in which Puzzle was nearly drowned trying to recover it, ends with a nature-defying (or -fulfilling) journey up that same waterfall: Tirian "moved his legs and arms as if he were swimming but he moved straight upwards: as if one could swim up the wall of a house" (157). What were largely night and darkness in the old Narnia have given way to everlasting day: Aslan declares, "The dream is ended: this is the morning" (165). What was a world with a beginning and an end has become one "which has always been here and always will be here . . . in Aslan's real world" (153–54). And what was a story with a beginning and an end, as this story is the "end" of the *Chronicles of Narnia*, through grace, breaks out of that "enclosure" and participates in the story that has no end. For, for those who reach Aslan's country it is "only the beginning of the real story. All their life in this world and all their adventures in Narnia had only been the cover and the title page: now at last they were beginning Chapter One of the Great Story which no one on earth has read: which goes on for ever: in which every chapter is better than the one before" (165).

# 12

## *Conclusion*

The books that make up the *Chronicles of Narnia* are so various that no all-embracing conclusion for them seems possible. And yet their very variety is the key to their power. The individuality of each and the multifariousness of them all testify to Lewis's delight in creation itself, as seen in the many different worlds of his imagination—Animal Land, Boxen, Puritania, Malacandra, Perelandra, the purlieus of heaven, Narnia, Glome. Lewis abhorred the limited vision of those who could not see our "nature" as one among many possible natures, each with its own peculiar personality, to be enjoyed as such *sub specie aeternitatis*, in the hand of God.[1] The nature of the creator, of imagined worlds or of our own, is one of endless renewal: "Never did He make two things the same; never did He utter one word twice."[2]

For Lewis this creative mutation was not only an expression of delight in the vastness of being itself, but also a *technique* for making the reader so aware. If our expectations are continually reversed, if our assumptions are continually proven false, the enclosures of our mental worlds will be broken down and we be made aware of how much larger "reality" is than any of our categorizations of it. Hence the constant displacements throughout *The Lion, the Witch and the*

111

*Wardrobe*, and why the sixth book of the series, *The Magician's Nephew*, is chronologically earlier than the first, describing the original creation of Narnia. There are different children to become used to from book to book, and different places—Narnia, a ship on an ocean, the land of Calormen, the "other" world of Charn. The experience is as described in William Wordsworth's "Intimations Ode," one of "fallings from us, vanishings"; or of the nature of the protagonist John's "mystic" vision in *The Pilgrim's Regress*, when "All the furniture of his mind was taken away."[3] Just so, the motifs of change and altered expectations that make up the *Chronicles of Narnia* can serve an evangelical purpose.

The uncertainty of our surroundings in the Narnia books reinforces another recurrent theme, that of the seemingly accidental turning out to be part of a pattern we were unaware of. The "fortuitous" arrival in Narnia via the wardrobe of the children in *The Lion* fulfills the prophecy concerning the Sons of Adam and Daughters of Eve, and the apparently random conjunction of Edmund, Aslan, and the witch makes up the pattern of Deep Magic that alone can destroy the witch and save Narnia. The "chance" events of *The Horse and His Boy* were directed by the immediate action of Aslan. The creation of Narnia in *The Magician's Nephew* could in a sense be said to have "waited on" the series of blunders that bring its first king and queen, together with the witch, to that land. The experience is something like that of Ransom in *Perelandra*, when he learns from a voice speaking to him by night that "it is not for nothing that you are named Ransom":

> The whole distinction between things accidental and things designed . . . was purely terrestrial. The pattern is so large that within the little frame of earthly experience there appear pieces of it between which we can see no connection, and other pieces between which we can. Hence we rightly, for our use, distinguish the accidental from the essential. But step outside that frame and the distinction drops down into the void, fluttering useless wings. He had been forced out of the frame, caught up into the larger pattern.[4]

This idea of being "taken out of oneself" is basic to the *Chronicles*. The little enclosed world of Narnia is "invaded" in *The Lion*, first by the children, then by Aslan and spring. What was a frozen world (parallel to a frozen mind), is awakened and renewed. In *The Last Battle* Narnia is "uncreated" only to open onto new and more "real" countries. We are often made to travel beyond Narnia, whether on the ocean of *The Voyage*, or to Harfang and Underland in *The Silver Chair*, or to Calormen and Archenland in *The Horse and His Boy*. The journey of the *Dawn Treader* links up the enclosed worlds of the various islands encountered en route. Shasta in *The Horse and His Boy* is taken out of himself through his travels and thereby discovers a new identity. The accent is always on spiritual growth out of the old self, symbolized in the way that Eustace in *The Voyage* is released from the dragon form of his own greed only by having the reptilian skin torn off down to its deepest layer. What is attacked throughout *Prince Caspian* is the enclosed self that refuses to acknowledge outside reality.

Great value is placed on meeting and society: the child protagonists are almost always shown in pairs or groups. In *The Lion* and *The Voyage* the quests link up the separated parts of a country, or the isolated egos on islands. Those who live alone or conceal things are either evil or at risk of becoming so—the witch, King Miraz, the Tisroc of Calormen, Prince Rilian in *The Silver Chair*. Nearly all the books involve a process of widening community, as all the talking animals and awakened trees come together again in *The Lion* and *Prince Caspian*, even as everyone comes together in death at the end of *The Last Battle*. In the witch in her castle in *The Lion*, or the enchantress of Underland in *The Silver Chair*, or the Tisroc sitting atop his city of Tashbaan in *The Horse and His Boy*, or the ape at his hut in *The Last Battle* we see evil as an absorptive center, drawing all it can into itself, whether freezing Narnia, binding Rilian, or enslaving the Narnians. By contrast Aslan radiates outward, whether in making or restoring life and community, or in pervading all creation with his presence.[5]

All these patterns can be traced throughout Lewis's fiction. Underlying them all is a desire to shake us loose from old certainties, to catch us up "into the larger pattern," so that we may experience a continual sense of that discomposing otherness that ultimately is located in God: "If we never met the dark, and the road that leads no-whither, and the question to which no answer is imaginable, we should have in our minds no likeness of the Abyss of the Father, into which if a creature drop down his thoughts for ever he shall hear no echo return to him."[6]

There is, it need hardly be said, a Christian pattern to the *Chronicles*, a pattern that for Lewis is precisely Christian in not being quite the pattern that we know, for here, in the sense of the order in which the books were written, the Passion, Redemption, and Resurrection take place "before" the creation of the world. And while there is a last judgment and a destruction of all Narnia, there is no fall of man or beast as we know it to explain the presence of evil in the world, only the arrival from outside of the wicked witch. Further, we may trace a certain circularity in that the restoration of Narnia accomplished by Aslan in *The Lion* is accomplished on another level, not through Aslan's death but through the death of old Narnia itself, in *The Last Battle*. But then, Narnia is continually having to be restored, protected, or given its innocence, whether in *Prince Caspian* or *The Horse and His Boy* or *The Magician's Nephew*. It seems a frailer world than ours. Its termination in *The Last Battle* seems brought about less by Aslan's fiat than through the fact that it has aged, has almost literally become a geriatric country. Indeed, Narnia, so animated through its talking animals and trees, is almost a creature in its own right; certainly it is an individuated nature like our own, as Lewis saw it. But Narnia is a shorter-breathed universe than ours (it has only about 2,500 years of history) and is somehow more fugitive. In the end, perhaps, its innermost spirit is like Lewis's "elusive bird" that it is the aim of the "net of story" to catch. For all the Narnia books, all the events and all the characters, are not simply elements in the construction of patterns, but are the celebration of a country, of a land, that from time to time harbors a spirit of innocence, a land on occasion permeated by the divine, a land that is one imperfect but affecting image of the Desirable that lies beyond all images and that drew Lewis to it all his Christian life.

> We do not want merely to *see* beauty, though, God knows, even that is bounty enough. We want something else which can hardly be put into words—to be united with the beauty we see, to pass

into it, to receive it into ourselves, to bathe in it, to become part of it. That is why we have peopled air and earth and water with gods and goddesses and nymphs and elves—that, though we cannot, yet these projections can, enjoy in themselves that beauty, grace, and power of which Nature is the image. . . . At present we are on the outside of the world, the wrong side of the door.[7]

# APPROACHES TO TEACHING

## DISCUSSION TOPICS FOR CHILDREN

1. What did you feel when Lucy got into a strange country through the wardrobe? Do you think it was a good idea to use a wardrobe? Why do you think the wardrobe is the third item in the title *The Lion, the Witch and the Wardrobe*?

2. Do you find the children in the books believable? Are they different from one another in character? Are they too good/ out of date/"high class"/English for you to sympathize with?

3. Do you think Lewis gives more place to boys than to girls in the stories?

4. Do you think Lewis is at all racially prejudiced, for example in the description of the Calormenes?

5. Do you find the battles and the deaths too violent, or not violent enough? (When the Narnia books came out in the 1950s, educationalists thought them too violent.)

6. Do you think Edmund's eating of Turkish Delight was a dreadful sin?

7. What do you think of Aslan? Is he a king, or is he something more? Why do you feel this way? What effect does his coming have on Narnia?

8. Why couldn't Aslan just destroy the witch? Didn't he have enough power? Why did he have to die?

9. What effect does Aslan's dying have? Did you think it "right" that he should then be able to come to life again?

10. Is there anything about Aslan's story here that reminds you

of any other story that you know? Do you think that the author intended you to be reminded of this other story? If so, how?

11. Was it a good idea to make Aslan a lion rather than, say, a man? Do you think it is done to appeal to our love of wild animals?

12. Would you say Aslan is a wild animal? Or is he a tame one?

13. Do you think Narnia is just a made-up world? If so, why do you feel our world is more real? What do you think of the way our world and Narnia lie close together beyond the door in *The Last Battle*?

14. Do you think putting an Edwardian lamppost from our world into Narnia was a good idea?

15. Do you think *The Lion, the Witch and the Wardrobe* stands on its own, or does it need a sequel? (Remember that when he wrote it Lewis had no intention of writing a series.)

16. Why do the children have to return to England at the end of every Narnia story, if no time passes in our world while they are in Narnia?

17. Do you find the evil characters more interesting or attractive than the good ones? Consider the witch in *The Lion*, or Jadis in *The Magician's Nephew*, or the enchantress in *The Silver Chair*, or the ape Shift or the cat Ginger in *The Last Battle*.

18. Why did Lewis use Narnia as his setting? Is it just another version of our world?

19. Why does Lewis have real-life children from modern times go to Narnia? (J. R. R. Tolkien in *The Hobbit* uses strange creatures from within the fantasy world as central characters.)

20. Do you have a clear picture of Narnia? And of the countries round about it?

21. Lewis called the Narnia stories fairy tales. Do you know any fairy tales? Do you think that what Lewis wrote is like them?

22. Are the Narnia books meant for a child? Or do you think it takes an older person to understand or appreciate them?

23. Do you think the Narnia books are actually written in praise of the childlike view of life?

24. Did you find it too much of a jolt when the children became High Kings and Queens of Narnia and were fighting battles—and then were turned back to children again?
25. Does Lewis understand what children are like? And what they like?
26. Do you think the stories are dated—too polite, respectful, moral?
27. If we read the Narnia books in their proper historical order, we would read *The Magician's Nephew* before *The Lion*, and *The Horse and His Boy* after *The Lion*. Do you think we should read the books this way?
28. What scene did you like best in *Prince Caspian*? Why?
29. When did you first guess that the children were back in Narnia?
30. How did you feel when you realized it was Narnia a thousand years from the time they had last visited it?
31. Do you think it is right that they should be ordinary children here after having been High Kings and Queens in Narnia in *The Lion*?
32. Is the story of this book at all like that of *The Lion*? If so, how?
33. Do you think this story is as original or as good as *The Lion*?
34. What is wrong with Eustace in *The Voyage of the "Dawn Treader"*? Why is he turned into a dragon?
35. Why are the Narnians sailing to the utter east in *The Voyage*? What do they want? What do you most want in life? Did that change after you read this book? Would you have preferred to stay at one of the islands?
36. Why is Aslan so often absent or hard to see, as in *Prince Caspian, The Voyage, The Silver Chair*, and *The Horse and His Boy*?
37. What is wrong with Experiment House at the beginning of *The Silver Chair*? Why does Lewis put this episode in; and return to it at the end?
38. Is the direction of the journey the children take in this story different from that in *The Voyage*? How?

39. What is the Marsh-wiggle like? Do you think he is the right companion for the children?
40. Rilian is found underground, shut in a room, and at times bound to a chair. Why?
41. Do you think *The Horse and His Boy* is quite different from the other Narnia stories? How?
42. Why are horses and people both at the center of *The Horse and His Boy*?
43. Aslan says he was with the band all along, helping them in other shapes. Can you accept this?
44. Do you think it was pure chance that led the children to Charn and later to Narnia in *The Magician's Nephew*? Was it an accident that they found and released Jadis? Was it pure chance that she came back with them to England and later to Narnia? Was it a coincidence that they arrived in Narnia just as Aslan was creating it?
45. What kinds of magic are there in *The Magician's Nephew*?
46. Can you accept a cabdriver and his wife as the first king and queen of Narnia?
47. Did Narnia have to end?
48. What do you think of the ape Shift and Puzzle the Donkey? Or of their being made the causes of the overthrow of Narnia?
49. How is Narnia in front of the stable door in *The Last Battle* different from Narnia beyond it?
50. In this story the children die and go to heaven. What do you think about this?

## USE OF SOURCES FOR COMPARISON

1. Put the story of Christ's Passion and Resurrection (e.g., Matthew 27, 28) beside those of Aslan in *The Lion* (135–49), and ask the children what they make of it. Is it simply a retelling, or is it a new story in a different world, though with the same basic divine pattern?
2. Similarly compare the Creation and the Fall stories in Genesis 1 (or Milton, *Paradise Lost*, books 7–10) with the creation

and averted fall in Narnia in *The Magician's Nephew,* 93–108, 143–53.

3. Put the ending of Narnia in *The Last Battle,* 135–43 beside the destruction of the world shown in Revelation.

4. Put the description of Ramandu visited by the bird in *The Voyage* 173–77 beside Isaiah 6:5–7; or of the lamb offering the children breakfast beside John 21:9–13; or of Shasta visited by the "Voice" in *The Horse and His Boy,* p. 139, beside Exodus 3:14; or of the ape Shift using a false Aslan to gain the allegiance of the Narnians in *The Last Battle* (29–35, 40–42) beside Matthew 24:23–24 on false Christs.

5. Put the episode of Mammon's cave with its silver chair in Spenser, *The Faerie Queene,* book II, canto 7, especially stanza 53, beside Rilian's seat in *The Silver Chair,* 140–46.

6. Compare Hans Christian Andersen, "The Snow Queen," with Narnia and the witch as they are described in *The Lion.*

7. Compare Edith Nesbit's account of the strange rules of amulet magic in *The Story of the Amulet* with the magic of the rings in *The Magician's Nephew;* or a passage from James Flecker's *Hassan* with the Calormene sections of *The Horse and His Boy.*

# PASSAGES TO READ OUT LOUD (In each case ask how the effect is achieved.)

1. Lucy first going through the wardrobe into Narnia in *The Lion,* pp. 11–15; or the witch meeting Edmund, anywhere from 32–40.

2. Read the passage describing Aslan surrounded by the Narnians, and then that of the witch with her followers, in *The Lion,* 115, 137–38. What are the differences between them?

3. The last stages of the journey in *The Voyage of the "Dawn Treader,"* 205–6. In what way does this affect you and why?

4. Meeting the Marsh-wiggle Puddleglum in *The Silver Chair,* 63–65.

5. The council in the Tisroc's palace in *The Horse and His Boy,*

95–97, for the different characters and the flavor of the Calormene idiom.

6. The destruction of Charn and the creation of Narnia in *The Magician's Nephew*, 55–61, 93–99, 104–6.
7. The beginning of *The Last Battle* with Shift and Puzzle, 9–10; or the end, with the journey toward Aslan's country, 156–57, 163–65; or the end of Narnia, 135–43.

## SECTIONS TO ACT OUT

1. The death and resurrection of Aslan in *The Lion*, pp. 136–41, 146–49. (The first should be easier. A narrator should read out the nondialogue sections from the book while the action is being performed. The main area should be dimly lit, preferably with a red or lurid green light. Everyone should have a speaking part and simply read it from the book. The helpless "Aslan" will be at the center, and all the others at first hesitant, then darting closer and closer, like bullies in a playground.)
2. The awakening of the stone animals in *The Lion*, 152–54. Get the children to hold a variety of (not uncomfortable) attitudes and then have "Aslan"—distinguished perhaps by yellow clothes, go round them waking them up. Again there should be voice-over narration.
3. Rilian in the chair in *The Silver Chair*, 141–46.
4. Shasta's encounter by night with the Voice in *The Horse and His Boy*, 137–40. Again the room should be near-dark, and the Voice perhaps come from behind a curtain.
5. The ringing by Digory of the little bell he finds on the table in the hall of living statues in Charn, in *The Magician's Nephew*, 49–53; the encounter of the witch and Aunt Letty on 76–77.

# NOTES AND REFERENCES

(Where no full reference is given, the item appears in the bibliography.)

## 1. Historical Context

1. C. S. Lewis, "*De Descriptione Temporum*," An Inaugural Lecture by the Professor of Medieval and Renaissance Literature at the University of Cambridge (Cambridge: Cambridge University Press, 1955). On Lewis's life and character, see his *Surprised by Joy*; Green and Hooper, *C. S. Lewis*; C. N. Manlove, *Modern Fantasy: Five Studies* (Cambridge: Cambridge University Press, 1975), 99–101; and A. N. Wilson, *C. S. Lewis*.

2. *Surprised by Joy, passim*; see also Manlove, 106–11.

3. Owen Barfield, Introduction to *Light on C. S. Lewis*, ed. Jocelyn Gibb (London: Geoffrey Bles, 1965), ix–xxi; Holbrook, *The Skeleton in the Wardrobe*, 118–27.

4. Wilson, 181, 191–92, 208, 245–46.

5. For a full account of the group, see Humphrey Carpenter, *The Inklings: C. S. Lewis, J. R. R. Tolkien, Charles Williams, and their Friends* (London: George Allen and Unwin, 1978).

6. Wilson, *C. S. Lewis*, 214.

7. *Surprised by Joy*, 187.

8. Ibid., 168–71.

9. Lewis is quite distinctive from Tolkien in his mixing of different worlds, his refusal of digression and detail, and his insistence on divine story rather than history in Narnia. In a letter of 15 May 1959 to Charles Moorman (*Letters of C. S. Lewis*, 287), Lewis said that Charles Williams was the only one of the Inklings to influence him.

10. Colin Manlove, *Christian Fantasy: From 1200 to the Present* (London: Macmillan, 1992), 253–61.

11. Lewis, ed., *George MacDonald: An Anthology* (London: Geoffrey Bles, 1946), says of such myth, "It goes beyond the expression of things we have already felt. It arouses in us sensations we have never had before, never anticipated having, as though we had broken out of our normal mode of consciousness and 'possessed joys not promised to our birth' " (16).

12. As portrayed in *Surprised by Joy.* The fullest of Lewis's essays on the whole subject of *Sehnsucht* is his "The Weight of Glory," *Transposition,* 21–33. On longing in the Narnia books and in Lewis's work generally, see Eliane Tixier, "Imagination Baptized, or, 'Holiness' in the *Chronicles of Narnia,*" *The Longing for a Form,* ed. Peter Schakel, 136–58; and Corbin Scott Carnell, *Bright Shadow of Reality: C. S. Lewis and the Feeling Intellect* (Grand Rapids, Mich.: Eerdmans, 1979).

13. See Manlove, *Christian Fantasy.*

# 2. The Importance of the Chronicles

1. Several major fantasies of the 1950s show the apparently small or negligible as important—Mary Norton's *The Borrowers* (1953), the Ring and the hobbits in *The Lord of the Rings* (1954–55), or the Wart in T. H. White's *The Once and Future King* (1958); and one could add the way the "simple" change of most people becoming blind causes societal collapse in John Wyndham's science fiction novel *The Day of the Triffids* (1951).

2. "Sometimes Fairy Stories May Say Best What's to Be Said," in *Of Other Worlds,* 38.

3. Wendy Holden, "Non-Vital Statistics in Minds of Americans," *Daily Telegraph,* 12 August 1989, 3.

# 3. Critical Reception

1. Wilson, *C. S. Lewis,* 222; Carpenter, *The Inklings,* 227–28.

2. Green and Hooper, *C. S. Lewis,* 239–40.

3. Letter of 5 March 1951 in *Letters of C. S. Lewis,* 228.

4. Green and Hooper, *C. S. Lewis,* 255.

5. Chad Walsh, "Impact on America," in *Light on C. S. Lewis*, 113.

6. The substance of this letter is quoted on the back cover of the 1973 book version of Lindskoog's thesis. Lewis had in fact met her in 1956.

7. Most of these are detailed in Christopher and Ostling's *Checklist*.

8. Preface to Kathryn Lindskoog, *The Lion of Judah in Never-Never Land*, 13.

# 4. Introduction

1. Wilson, *C. S. Lewis*, 211–30, esp. 225.

2. "It All Began with a Picture . . ." (1960), in *Of Other Worlds*, 42.

3. Wilson, 220.

4. Green and Hooper, *C. S. Lewis*, 245.

5. "Sometimes Fairy Stories May Say Best What's to Be Said," in *Of Other Worlds*, 36; see also 37.

6. *Perelandra*, 166. Compare letter of 29 December 1958 in *Letters of C. S. Lewis*, 283: "[Aslan] is an invention giving an imaginary answer to the question, 'What might Christ become like, if there really were a world like Narnia and He chose to be incarnate and die and rise again in *that* world as he actually has done in ours?' This is not allegory at all. So in *Perelandra*." For more on this subject, see Charles A. Huttar, "C. S. Lewis's Narnia and the 'Grand Design,' " in Schakel, ed., *The Longing for a Form*, 119–35.

7. "Sometimes Fairy Stories May Say Best What's to Be Said," in *Of Other Worlds*, 36–37.

8. "On Stories," in *Of Other Worlds*, 20–21.

# 5. The Lion, the Witch and the Wardrobe

1. "When I wrote the *Lion* I had no notion of writing the others" (Letter of 2 December 1962 in *Letters of C. S. Lewis*, 307).

2. As by Green and Hooper, *C. S. Lewis*, 241; Peter Schakel, *Reading with the Heart*, 140 n.24; Donald E. Glover, *C. S. Lewis*, 241. Compare, however, Wilson, *C. S. Lewis*, 221.

3. George MacDonald, "The Golden Key" (1867), in *The Light Princess and Other Tales* (London: Victor Gollancz, 1967), 238.

# 6. Prince Caspian

1. J. R. R. Tolkien, *Tree and Leaf*, 53.
2. Ibid., 63.

# 7. The Voyage of the "Dawn Treader."

1. Derived from the Monocoli or Umbrella-footed of Pliny's *Natural History*, VII, 23.
2. There is a sense in which the children mature and begin to interact presexually without ceasing to be children during the *Chronicles*. Certainly in the next three books we have not a group of children but a single boy and girl working together.
3. The reference is to Isaiah 6:5–7 and to the coal of fire that, laid on the lips of the prophet, purges his spirit and enables him to preach.
4. "The Weight of Glory," in *Transposition*, 23–26.
5. This is the way Lewis saw it in "The Weight of Glory": "At first sight it chills, rather than awakes, my desire. And that is just what I ought to expect" (*Transposition*, 26).

# 8. The Silver Chair

1. This school is founded on the kinds of "Freudian" behaviorist premises that Lewis always detested: he attacks Freud as "Sigismund Enlightenment" in *The Pilgrim's Regress*, 57–60.
2. John D. Cox, "Epistemological Release in *The Silver Chair*," in Schakel, ed. *The Longing for a Form*, 159–68, discusses the motif of reality's true nature throughout the story.
3. For instance, in his remarks that Caspian may not live long, that

Trumpkin the dwarf is too old for the job of regent, and that he and the children will be attacked by enemies (67).

4. See also Cox, "Epistemological Release," in *The Longing for a Form*, ed. Schakel, 161.

5. Northrop Frye, *The Secular Scripture: A Study of the Structure of Romance* (Cambridge, Mass.: Harvard University Press, 1976), 97, 129; cited in Schakel, *Reading with the Heart*, 65, 73, 76.

6. By Schakel in *Reading with the Heart*, 65.

# 9. The Horse and His Boy

1. Lewis first read *Hassan* in 1923 and recorded that "It made a great impression on me and I believe it is really a great work" (*All My Road Before Me*, 278).

2. Schakel, *Reading with the Heart*, 82–83, linking Narnia with the desire for heaven described in "The Weight of Glory."

3. On the theme of growth into true identity throughout the story, see Schakel, *Reading with the Heart*, 85–96.

4. Though the title was only one of a number of substitutes put up by Lewis when the publisher, Geoffrey Bles, did not like his first, *Narnia and the North* (Green and Hooper, *C. S. Lewis*, 245).

# 10. The Magician's Nephew

1. See Green and Hooper, *C. S. Lewis*, 248.

2. Ibid., 242–43, 247–48.

3. *Perelandra*, 246–47.

# 11. The Last Battle

1. Glover, *C. S. Lewis*, 181, 186, has a similar view.

2. This is very similar to the process that is followed toward the eventual

realization of the truth about herself by the sinful Orual in *Till We Have Faces*, also published in 1956; see also Manlove, *C. S. Lewis*, 202–6.

## 12. Conclusion

1. *Miracles*, 79–81.
2. *Perelandra*, 246.
3. *The Pilgrim's Regress*, 24.
4. *Perelandra*, 168.
5. See Manlove, *C. S. Lewis*, and *Christian Fantasy*, 242–50.
6. *Perelandra*, 251.
7. "The Weight of Glory," in *Transposition*, 31.

# SELECTED BIBLIOGRAPHY

## Primary Works

### Books

*The Pilgrim's Regress: An Allegorical Apology for Christianity, Reason and Romanticism*. London: J. M. Dent, 1933. With author's preface and notes, London: Geoffrey Bles, 1943.

*Out of the Silent Planet*. London: John Lane, Bodley Head, 1938.

*The Problem of Pain*. London: Centenary Press, 1940.

*Perelandra: A Novel*. London: John Lane, Bodley Head, 1943.

*That Hideous Strength: A Modern Fairy-Tale for Grown-ups*. London: John Lane, Bodley Head, 1945.

*The Great Divorce: A Dream*. London: Geoffrey Bles, Centenary Press, 1945.

*Miracles: A Preliminary Study*. London: Geoffrey Bles, Centenary Press, 1947.

*"Transposition" and Other Addresses*. London: Geoffrey Bles, 1949. Contains "The Weight of Glory" (1941).

*The Chronicles of Narnia:*
   *The Lion, the Witch and the Wardrobe: A Story for Children*. London: Geoffrey Bles, 1950.
   *Prince Caspian: The Return to Narnia*. London: Geoffrey Bles, 1951.
   *The Voyage of the "Dawn Treader."* London: Geoffrey Bles, 1952.
   *The Silver Chair*. London: Geoffrey Bles, 1953.
   *The Horse and His Boy*. London: Geoffrey Bles, 1954.
   *The Magician's Nephew*. London: Bodley Head, 1955.
   *The Last Battle: A Story for Children*. London: Bodley Head, 1956.

*Mere Christianity*. London: Geoffrey Bles, 1952.

*Surprised by Joy: The Shape of My Early Life*. London: Geoffrey Bles, 1955.

*Till We Have Faces: A Myth Retold*. London: Geoffrey Bles, 1956.

*Letters of C. S. Lewis* (ed. W. H. Lewis). London: Geoffrey Bles, 1966.

*Of Other Worlds: Essays and Stories* (ed. Walter Hooper). London: Geoffrey Bles, 1966. Contains "On Stories" (1947), "On Three Ways of Writing for Children" (1952), "Sometimes Fairy Stories May Say Best What's to Be Said" (1956), "On Juvenile Tastes" (1958), and "It All Began with a Picture . . ." (1960).

*"The Dark Tower" and Other Stories* (ed. Walter Hooper). London: Collins, 1977.

*Boxen: The Imaginary World of the Young C. S. Lewis* (ed. Walter Hooper). London: Collins, 1985.

*Letters to Children* (eds. Lyle W. Dorsett and Marjorie Lamp Mead). New York: Macmillan, 1985.

*All My Road Before Me: The Diary of C. S. Lewis, 1922–1927* (ed. Walter Hooper). London: Geoffrey Bles, 1991.

## Secondary Works

### Biographical and Critical Studies

Christopher, Joe R. *C. S. Lewis*. Twayne's English Authors Series, no. 442. Boston: G. K. Hall, 1977. Rather thin on the *Chronicles of Narnia*; too much pursuit of Tolkienian parallels.

Christopher, Joe R., and Joan K. Ostling, eds. *C. S. Lewis: An Annotated Checklist of Writings About Him and His Works*. Kent, Ohio: Kent State University Press, 1974. Excellent annotated reviews both of individual Narnia books and of the *Chronicles* as a whole up to 1972; indispensable.

Gibson, Evan K. *C. S. Lewis, Spinner of Tales: A Guide to His Fiction*. Washington, D.C.: Christian University Press, 1980. An enthusiastic book for the beginner, but apart from the odd insight, no more than a straightforward and uncritical appreciation.

Glover, Donald E. *C. S. Lewis: The Art of Enchantment*. Athens, Ohio: Ohio University Press, 1981. A thorough investigation of each of the tales, commenting on their literary features rather than simply their content or themes; many insights; marred by a rather limp approach and oversubjective judgments.

Green, Roger Lancelyn, and Walter Hooper. *C. S. Lewis: A Biography*. London: Collins, 1974. Good for the comments by Hooper on the origins of the Narnia books and the history of their composition and publication, though generally a hagiographic treatment. Otherwise superseded by Wilson (see below).

# Selected Bibliography

Holbrook, David. *The Skeleton in the Wardrobe: C. S. Lewis's Fantasies: A Phenomenological Study* (Lewisburg, Pa.: Bucknell University Press, 1991). Contains an exhaustively Freudian reading of the *Chronicles*.

Hooper, Walter. *Past Watchful Dragons: The Narnian Chronicles of C. S. Lewis*. New York: Collier, 1979. A general survey of the origins, background, nature, and "Christian" significance of the *Chronicles*, most useful for the early fragments of Narnia material from Lewis's notebooks, discussed in its chapter 5.

Howard, Thomas. *The Achievement of C. S. Lewis*. Wheaton, Ill.: Harold Shaw, 1980. A 30-page chapter discusses the character of Narnia more than of the books themselves. Overpersonal and polemical; written from a Christian standpoint.

Kilby, Clyde S. *The Christian World of C. S. Lewis*. Abingdon, Berks.: Marcham Manor Press, 1965. The first general introduction to all Lewis's work: the chapter on the Narnia books is mostly narrational, followed by brief comments on different aspects. For the beginner only.

Lindskoog, Kathryn. *The Lion of Judah in Never-Never Land: The Theology of C. S. Lewis Expressed in His Fantasies for Children*. Grand Rapids, Mich.: Eerdmans, 1973. An excellent account that relates the *Chronicles of Narnia* to the rest of Lewis's work and to his sources, widening understanding of many aspects of the books.

Manlove, C. N. *C. S. Lewis: His Literary Achievement*. London: Macmillan, 1987. Detailed literary and thematic investigations of the Narnia books. Shows them organized by many subtle patterns. Sometimes a bit too minute and overintellectual in approach.

Murphy, Brian. *C. S. Lewis*. Starmont Reader's Guide, no. 14. Mercer Island, Wash: Starmont House, 1983. Brief account of the Narnia books, pithily expressed by an able mind.

Schakel, Peter J. *Reading with the Heart: The Way into Narnia*. Grand Rapids, Mich.: Eerdmans, 1979. The first and probably still the best account of the Narnia books as literature, if rather more interested in thematic patterning than in style itself.

———, ed. *The Longing for a Form: Essays on the Fiction of C. S. Lewis*. Grand Rapids, Mich: Baker, 1977. Contains a section with four essays on the *Chronicles of Narnia* (discussed under "Critical Reception," chap. 3, pp. 15–16 above).

Tolkien, J. R. R. "On Fairy-Stories" (1938–39). Repr. and enl. in *Tree and Leaf*. London: Allen and Unwin, 1964. Invaluable both in comparison to and as possible source for some of Lewis's views on fantasy and "sub-creation."

Walsh, Chad. *The Literary Legacy of C. S. Lewis.* London: Sheldon Press, 1979. The thirty-five-page section on three of the Narnia books is largely narrative, with occasional (shrewd) comment.

Wilson, A. N. *C. S. Lewis: A Biography.* London: Collins, 1990. Undoubtedly the best biography, at once affectionate and critical and written with considerable urbanity. The account of the origins and nature of the Narnia books in Lewis's experience is both original and convincing.

# $I_{ndex}$

# Index

# THE AUTHOR

Colin Manlove (b. 1942) is Reader in English Literature at the University of Edinburgh, Scotland, and author of *Modern Fantasy: Five Studies* (1975), *Literature and Reality 1600–1800* (1978), *The Gap in Shakespeare: The Motif of Division from "Richard II" to "The Tempest"* (1981), *The Impulse of Fantasy Literature* (1983), *Science Fiction: Ten Explorations* (1986), *C. S. Lewis: His Literary Achievement* (1987), *Critical Thinking: A Guide to Interpreting Literary Texts* (1989), and *Christian Fantasy: From 1200 to the Present* (1992), as well as numerous essays and articles. His particular interest in the fiction of C. S. Lewis is seen in a section of his *Modern Fantasy*, in *C. S. Lewis*, and in a chapter of *Christian Fantasy*. His main literary interest has been in the fantasy and science fiction area, in which he currently teaches an honors course. He received the Distinguished Scholarship Award of the International Association for the Fantastic in the Arts at its Tenth Anniversary Conference in Florida in 1989. In 1990 the University of Edinburgh awarded him the degree of D.Litt. for his work on fantasy literature. He lives in Edinburgh with his wife, Evelyn. They have two university-age sons, John and David.

14.95

823 Lewis M
Manlove, C. N.
The chronicles of Narnia.